**Basic Office
Systems & Records**

Basic Office Systems & Records

GERARD TAVERNIER

Gower Press

First published in Great Britain by
Gower Press Limited, Epping, Essex
1972

© Gower Press Limited 1972
ISBN 0 7161 0138 6

Computerised origination by
Autoset, Brentwood, Essex.

Printed in Great Britain by
Redwood Press Limited
Trowbridge, Wiltshire

Contents

Illustrations

Introduction

The enormous increase in paperwork that firms of all sizes have experienced in recent years has frequently created clerical work out of all proportion with the size of the turnover or the number of employees on the payroll. It sometimes seems as if every request for information leads to the introduction of a new form.

Clearly there comes a time when any organisation must take a close hard look at the records and forms used for obtaining, processing and reporting data. Smaller organisations may feel that the cost of the few basic forms they use is negligible, but the real point is the cost of processing them—typing, duplication, reading, filing and storage.

It is the design of forms for easier processing, which needs analysis and on which we have concentrated in this book.

It is not necessarily fewer forms that are needed but a rational system for processing them—a system that will improve efficiency and productivity of the office staff. It should simplify the paperwork and help to distribute the clerical workload more evenly. It should help to eliminate bottlenecks and reduce discrepancies and the possibility of errors. It should help to establish better communication. It should relieve managers of the routine tasks and of the necessity to keep day by day checks on the work of their departments and enable them to concentrate instead on tasks more crucial to the success of the enterprise.

There is no simple or spectacular scheme for achieving all this. Every firm has its own needs and its own working environment and, for lack of a better word, style. But basically a well devised records system possesses a high degree of control, while still retaining the necessary flexibility to meet changing circumstances. It should furthermore be designed to provide the required information easily and regularly. The most important person in the company, the customer, is peculiarly liable to request information, sometimes on long distance telephone calls, and the information must be found quickly. It is irritating for a customer on the telephone or at a retail counter to wait while his credit facilities or his original order or even prices are being checked.

In the same way, the information contained on the records should be easily accessible for compiling reports. The system should be able to provide data in a number of ways to enable a variety of analysis and reports to be prepared without unnecessary effort. In many firms requests for statistical information tend to be piecemeal. perhaps as a result of some immediate need, and considerable time and effort are required to co-ordinate the data.

Of course it is not suggested that this book alone will give the precise method or a ready-made system which can simply be implemented in each individual company. It is fairly certain, however, that the approaches and the experience of the companies described in this book will provide the necessary impetus and, in addition, proper guidelines for developing similar systems with equal success.

Acknowledgements

For their advice and assistance in obtaining examples of forms to illustrate the principles advocated in the text I am grateful and indebted to

George Anson and Company
Kalamazoo Business Forms
Lamson Paragon
Oce-Skycopy Limited
Wiggins Teape Limited

Grateful acknowledgement is also made to the firms who have allowed their forms to be used as illustrations and to the Business Equipment Trade Association, the Department of Employment, the Department of Health and Social Security, the Inland Revenue, and to the US Government Small Administration for their assistance.

May I also thank Peter Baily, author and lecturer on purchasing and stock control and a member of the faculty at Glamorgan Polytechnic; Leslie Robinson, consultant on road transport management; Eric Oliver, security adviser to Unilever Limited, and John Wilson, company security officer at Yorkshire Imperial Metals Limited, whose ideas on the subject of record keeping which have been previously published have been used in this book.

Publisher's Note

The illustrative material in this book is drawn from actual documents used by companies, to whom acknowledgements are expressed in the captions, as well as from official forms available from government departments.

The need for a standard format in book reproduction means that the size and proportion of many documents have had to be modified. The essential information carried by each form, however, remains unaltered. Firms using this book to design or adapt their own systems and records will, of course, draw up forms of a shape and size to suit their own equipment and requirements, adding appropriate data covering company name, reference numbers, dates, specific instructions, and so on.

In describing specific government forms and records it has been necessary to refer to the statutory obligations on employers for completing and keeping these records. It should be stressed, however, that these references are intended simply as a guide and should not be treated as complete or as authoritative statements of the law. The law applies differently to different types of firms and industries and in various circumstances and there are exceptions to most regulations.

More detailed information regarding any statutory obligations referred to in this book may be obtained from official publications available free of charge from the relevant government offices. Leaflets concerning the Contracts of Employment Act, redundancy payments and other aspects of employment may be obtained from the local Employment Exchanges or the Department of Employment, 8 St James's Square, London, SW1. An employer's guide to the Pay As You Earn scheme may be obtained from any local office of the Inland Revenue. Employer's guides to flat rate and graduated national insurance contributions and contracted-out employment, industrial injuries and family allowance schemes, workmen's compensation and supplementary benefits may be obtained from any local office of the Department of Health and Social Security or from the Department's headquarters at Alexander Fleming House, Elephant and Castle, London, SE1.

1

Principles of Record Keeping

There are some basic principles which hold true for all systems and it is useful to start by examining these.

First, an information system should provide a high degree of control but, at the same time, must retain the necessary flexibility to meet the changing circumstances. It should be planned for expansion and designed so that it can be readily transferred to electronic or computerised data processing equipment should it ever be required.

The usefulness and therefore the effectiveness of the data obtained from a system can be best assessed by three main factors:

1   *Relevance.* The data recorded should be only that which is necessary for controlling company operations and testing their effectiveness and no more. What is needed is not more but less and better data.
2   *Timeliness.* The data must be made available in sufficient time and at the right frequency to enable the appropriate decisions to be made.
3   *Accuracy.* To be useful, data must be accurate, of course, but this does not mean it must always be 100 per cent accurate. To obtain precise data is costly and time consuming, resulting in delays. It is only necessary for data to be accurate enough to ensure that decisions based on it are more likely to be right than wrong. Data that is acquired in a routine way should be sufficient for most purposes.

Analysing the existing system

The office system must be looked at as a whole, not just the parts of it carried out by one person or section. There is no advantage in improving one operation if it is to create more work elsewhere.

In order to identify the problems and the potential areas of improvement it may be useful to define the functional structure of the organisation and the existing clerical procedures, including those performed outside the office. The object is to discover what is being done—and what is not being done—how it is done and why it is done in that way, what information is being provided and how it is used.

From this it will be possible to determine what information is needed in the first place, by whom and when. Then the most suitable procedures can be devised and documents designed for the most efficient dissemination of the information required.

It may be useful to define existing procedures in very simple flow process charts, showing the sequence of all operations, movements and delays which occur in a procedure or series of procedures, the documents used at each stage, and perhaps the clerks who carry out each stage of the procedure as well as the equipment used. The data each person receives and the information needed to assist them in controlling their activities should be given in detail. This is the clearest way of showing how one procedure affects another, the interaction of various forms, what information is copied from one form to another, and what use is made of various copies.

The whole system and each step in the process should them be analysed. If changes in established procedures are to be successful, it is a good idea at this stage to consult the staff involved in processing or using forms to discuss what data is wanted, when they need it and how is should be presented.

The critical questions to be asked throughout the analysis are: what, where, when, who and how? Can a procedure or form be modified in any way or dispensed with altogether? Circumstances change all the time and quite often work is carried out simply 'because it has always been done that way' and arrangements continue to be followed even though they may have become quite unsuitable or unnecessary. No procedure should be left unchallenged:

> Why is that done?
> Why in that place?
> Why by that person?
> Who else could do it?
> Could someone less qualified or skilled perhaps handle some of the details?
> Why is a procedure done in that sequence?
> What different sequence or timing could be tried?
> How else can its function be performed?
> Could a memo or entry on a blackboard or chart be used instead?
> Could the operation be combined with some different activity?
> Could it be eliminated?
> What is the worst thing that could happen if it were eliminated?

It is frequently possible to combine one form with another and have it serve the function of two or more. Several examples of this are shown in the appropriate chapers of the book. Similarly, copies of a form can sometimes be eliminated. It may be found sufficient merely to circulate rather than to copy individual forms which are neither urgent nor permanent value, though care must be taken to ensure that this does not cause constant queries.

The physical working arrangements should also be carefully checked:

Is the office layout satisfactory?
Is it possible to reduce the amount of time spent in walking or looking for information?
Could an operation be relocated nearer the next operation?
Can the distribution of documents be facilitated?
Is there an easier, safer or quicker way?
Why is that medium or equipment used?
Could it be partly mechanised?

It should be mentioned here that most reputable manufacturers of business forms and office equipment will normally undertake a study of company records and office systems without charge, though their objectivity in recommending the most appropriate systems and equipment may be questioned.

Companies without a computer may find it worth using computer bureaux or time-sharing facilities for such applications as accounts, payroll etc. Computer bureaux services can cover any of the operations involved in computerised records, from programming or data preparation to the running of the whole installation, with all the management responsibilities and problems which these entail.

When analysing the forms used, it is a good idea to list every form and its primary objective, the specific information it is intended to provide or action it is intended to initiate, and its potential functions. The list must include all forms that are stored. It may be that whole files of records are being stored and taking up valuable space because of one bit of information contained in them which could be included on some other record.

In larger firms, it may be useful to have managers note the relevance of each form on a checklist. Figure 1.1 is an example of such a checklist. All the data elements can then be arranged in a matrix to see the pattern of information which should be gathered and disseminated.

Many firms believe in sending a copy of everything to everyone who may be interested, on the premise that too much information is better than not enough. This is of doubtful validity.

Aspects of form design

Layout, type face, size, paper, colour help to produce a company image. A well designed form, however, is not only aesthetically pleasing, it must also be functional.

The design of forms depends very much on the way they are processed and the objectives of the information system. In most firms, allied functions require interrelated documents that bear to a large extent identical information and it may be that forms can be designed so that several can be completed at one writing. Unwarranted data can be omitted on some parts and space provided for additional data on others. This can save considerable time and labour and can obviate the need for transcribing, with the risk of errors and the tedious checking which this entails. Several examples of sets of forms are illustrated in the appropriate chapters.

Layout of forms.   Basically a form should be designed so that it can be completed easily with the minimum of writing and can be easily understood. Whenever possible it should be completed in natural sequence from left to right and from top to bottom. This helps to ensure that no necessary item is omitted. But there are other considerations. Items which are *always* filled in are best located at the left of forms; items which are not always completed in the middle and those which are seldom filled in at the right. This saves time when completing the form.

At the same time an effort should be made to place items logically according to the sequence of each operation. If the form is used in conjunction with another form, for instance, or if data is transferred from one form to another, as in the case of requisitions and purchase orders or applications and personnel records, the two forms should be designed together.

Every form should be easily identified and be self-explanatory. The purpose of the form should be prominently displayed at the top. This is particularly important for forms used or completed outside the organisation, by suppliers and job applicants for example.

The main item of identification–name of the employee, customer or supplier, order number and so on–should be placed wherever it can be most easily seen without having to draw the entire form from the file. This will speed up searching for the particular documents wanted. Filing margins, where needed, pre-punched holes, a light rule to show where a form should be folded can all help in the dispostion of forms.

The British Standards Institution recommends a margin of at least 23mm running the full length of a form at the left edge to facilitate filing without obscuring details. This margin could be used for printing instructions or other similar matter relevant to the form. Conditions of purchase could be printed there, for instance.

Spacing.   The correct spacing on forms is important but often neglected. It is not uncommon to see a form with a three or four inch space for age and a space for signature that would hardly accomodate initials.

Space for typewritten entries is straightforward. For vertical spacing there are five lines to 20mm or six line to one inch. Horizontal spacing depends on the size of type. Petit roman, the smallest type used on normal office typewriters, gives ten letters to 16mm, or sixteen letters to the inch. The two standard type sizes are elite and pica. Elite gives ten letters to 20mm or twelve letters to one inch; pica gives ten letters to 25mm or one inch. The space required for handwritten entries is obviously less straightforward. However, four lines vertically and eight lines horizontally to 25mm (1 inch) may be taken as a rough guide.

Paper size.   After studying all requirements, it is advisable to liaise with the printer to ensure the most economical cut of paper and to take advantage of standard size wherever possible. The size selected must satisfy office machine requirements and be suitable for existing filing equipment. The size of form should also be standardised as much as possible to reduce the variety of envelopes which have to be stocked.

The odd collection of Imperial sizes—foolscap, quarto, octavo and so on, is being replaced by the international metric systems in which the various sizes have a logical relationship. There is only one standard instead of the three of four found in the traditional British dimensions. This means that metric size stationery is cheaper to make and print.

The international sizes are based on one square metre of trimmed paper (841 x 1189mm) as shown in Figure 1.2. The standard range, with inch equivalents, is as follows:

	millimetres		inches				millimetres		inches		
2A	1189 X 1682		46.81 X	66.22		A5	148 X 210		5.83 X	8.27
A0	841 X 1189		33.11 X	46.81		A6	105 X 148		4.13 X	5.83
A1	594 X 841		23.39 X	33.11		A7	74 X 105		2.91 X	4.13
A2	420 X 594		16.54 X	23.39		A8	52 X 74		2.05 X	2.91
A3	297 X 420		11.69 X	16.54		A9	37 X 52		1.46 X	2.05
A4	210 X 297		8.27 X	11.69		A10	26 X 37		1.02 X	1.46

Normally A4 is the largest form size used; it can be accommodated in a standard typewriter. A5 is comparable to octavo and, along with A4 is the most commonly used for letterheads. It is also a popular size for invoices, statements, order forms and so on. A6 is known as the postcard size and is a smaller alternative for memos and receipts.

Some firms use two-thirds A4 size rather than the A5, a size which the British Standards Institution has now recognised. It has the advantage that one envelope can be used for both A4 and two-thirds A4, the former folded twice and the latter once. Moreover, the one die and block can be used to print both.

Figure 1.3 shows how an A1 sheet of paper can be cut most economically. It also illustrates how only one or two different size envelopes can be used to accomodate a variety of forms, another good reason why the new international sizes should be adopted wherever possible.

Envelope size. The most popular of the recommended metric envelope sizes are:

	millimetres			inches		
C4	299 X	325		9.02 X	12.76
C5	162 X	229		6.38 X	9.02
C6	114 X	162		4.49 X	6.38
DL	110 X	220		4.33 X	8.66

Of these the C6 and DL sizes are within the Post Office Preferred (POP) range. It is likely however, that the traditional British Imperial size envelopes will remain available for several more years, depending on demand. Those within the POP range are likely to be retained indefinitely.

On the subject of envelopes it may be pertinent to consider the feasibility of using window envelopes. They cost more than normal envelopes but the difference can usually be justified in time saved. To begin with, the name and address do not have to be typed on the envelope.

Another small bonus that cannot be ignored is that the letter or form cannot be inadvertently placed in the wrong envelope.

Legibility.   Distinctive coloured paper should be used for each copy of a form for easy recognition and to facilitate routing. In this connection it should be remembered that different colours cannot be shown on documents made on copiers and each should therefore also be identified.

It is also important that entries are legible on each copy in order to avoid confusion or delays. In general, about six copies can be obtained on forms completed on a typewriter, twelve on electric typewriters, and four by hand.

Paper weight (sometimes called substance) also affects copying power; quite a small change in weight can have significant effect.

Registration.   In making copies it is essential to obtain proper registration to avoid any data being obliterated, which is a good reason for avoiding bold rules. Multi-sets (see Figure 3.1 and 4.2 for example) and registers help to ensure proper registration. Each sheet is secured at the top with a carbon between. On completion of the entries the forms and carbons are snapped apart for distribution. If necessary, some of the copies can be left intact after the initial entries are made and re-inserted into the typwriter for subsequent entries without any loss of registration despite repeated handling. Also available, though little used, are the fanfold forms which are tied at the sides and head and foot to ensure an even better hold.

Standard forms.   Specialists printers of business forms offer a wide range of standard or stock forms designed for use in different types of industries and in many applications. Some firms have standard body layouts providing for the inclusion of special wording for the various column headings to suit a company's own particular requirements. It is much more economical to over-print a standard form than to try to change the basic design. In general however once a supply of forms reaches 2000 it is just as economical to have a specially designed form. And once the printing plates have been made, additional print runs are cheaper.

There are many forms, particularly those used within the company, which can be printed internally on duplicating or offset printing equipment. In this way, forms can be printed when needed, less capital is tied up in stationery stock and purchase tax (30 per cent) is avoided.

Function and design of filing systems

Basically, there are two points to keep in mind when devising a filing system. First the main reason for filing documents is so that they can be retrieved. The system should bring to light any individual record when it requires attention, and keep it outstanding until it has been taken care of. Conversely, records with missing information should not be fully buried in the files until that information is provided. If the data is not available at the time a form is made out, precaution should be taken that it is filled in when available.

The second important characteristic of a well devised system is its ability to provide comprehensive data about a complete activity, set-up, organisation and so on. Data should be easily available in a number of ways for preparing analyses and reports. Thus it is as well to know before establishing a filing system the sort of data which is most likely to be required. In many firms, requests for information or statistics tend to be piecemeal and considerable time and effort is required to co-ordinate the desired data. Very often management does without the necessary data and wrong decisions or, equally bad, no decisions are made.

In choosing filing equipment, there are four main factors to consider:

1 *Compactness*—The amount of office space required in relation to the quantity of information stored
2 *Mobility*—Can the information be moved from one place to another if necessary?
3 *Accessibility*—Are the files easy to refer to?
4 *Flexibility*—Can the documents be easily removed? Can additions and deletions be made without distrubing the sequence?

Indexing methods

Basically there are five methods of indexing: alphabetical, numerical, by subject, geographical and chronological.

Alphabetical indexing. This is the most widely used system of all for two main reasons: the ease in finding the information and the advantage of having all documents dealing with one subject, a supplier or a customer, for example, filed together. The sequence should be based on the key name or word according to the alphabet and nothing should come before it. Numbers are treated as though spelled out, so that the 600 Group for example would be filed under S.

Numerical indexing. This is probably the easiest method. There is never a problem of spelling or deciding on the proper sequence. Furthermore, continuous numbering provides a degree of security in that missing files are are noticed quickly. The main disadvantage is that the contents in the folders are not obvious, and a card index may be necessary. Numerical filing is used for documents numbered consecutively or when suppliers or customers for instance are given a code number. Different coloured tabs can be used to divide the folders in groups of 50 to 100. Tabs are often staggered from left to right so that a gap in the sequence is readily apparent.

When the numbered documents are unrelated to one another, they can be filed by terminal digit which means filing the document by reading the order number backward. The document numbered 123456, for example, is broken down like this:

56: cabinet or drawer number

34: folder number

12: paper number

This system makes it much easier to retrieve material and spreads the papers more evenly throughout the file. The same principle can be used in another way:

12: folder number

34: cabinet or drawer number

56: paper number

This method places 100 consecutive numbered documents together in a group, making it easier to file or retrieve 100 consecutively numbered documents at one time.

Indexing by subject.   Often used for quotation files, this method is particularly useful if the content of the documents is more important than from whom or to whom they pass. Subject filing is considered difficult because of the decisions which must be made constantly and consistently. It is best to arrange the topics and file headings in alphabetical order and have an index list accessible.

Indexing geographically.   This method is normally used only when location is a predominant factor. Customers' records, for example, can be divided in this way so that salesmen can look up those customers in the same district. Some contractors and suppliers will provide a delivery service only within a specific area, and records of vendors can be filed according to points of delivery.

Chronological indexing.   In this way folders are filed according to the date received or the date on which they require attention. The method can be used, for example, to remind customers when they need to have their equipment serviced. This is particularly useful when the business is slow. Similarly, one can identify past customers who are due to buy a new model. Sales are not only improved but so is the quality of the old purchase traded-in.

Mixed methods.   The combination of any of these methods is possible, of course. For example, in the larger alphabetical files a different number can be used for different divisions of the alphabetical sequence. The number 50 may be used to divide all folders filed under E and a first digit added to indicate the second letter of the alphabet, so that 50–1 would be Ea and 50–2 would be Eb. With this method, documents may still be called by name but it is much easier to file the refile them even though the documents themselves are not numbered.

Methods of data retrieval

Virtually every piece of information held on a record can be coded in some way for identification, either for carrying out statistical analyses or for individual attention. Personnel records, for example, can be coded to indicate particular experience and skills, or those ready for training, worthy of promotion or approaching retirement. Purchase orders can be signalled to indicate the expected delivery date. Many other examples are given in the appropriate chapters, but care must be taken to ensure that the coding system does not become so sophisticated that the whole set-up becomes unwieldy.

Coding.   One way of coding is with labels or tabs of various colours and shapes to denote characteristics or attributions on the record. Statistical analysis is simplified even more if the cards are staggered in some way so that they overlap each other to form an index. Cards are staggered in echelon fashion on parallel guide rails revealing only the edge of each card. Key characteristics are indicated on the leading edge by inserting different coloured tabs in cellulose or acetate strips (see Figure 5.8). Even the most cursory examination will give a good picture of the entire file.

Edge and body-punched cards.   Forms printed on heavy stock may be coded by holes punched in the body or the edge of the card and selected by means of spindles or rods. There are many such forms on the market designed for general use in various functions. Basically there are three types—slotted, notched and edge-punched cards. In all three types, holes are punched in predetermined spaces to designate the particular characteristics by which the cards may be sorted. In this way, it is possible to select cards with one or several characteristics in common.

In the first type, the holes are slotted in the body of the card. The features are represented by 'positions between two holes'. The holes are then connected to form slots about 10mm long, if the items recorded on the card possess the features represented by the positions. The advantage of this type over the others is that the slot allows the cards to fall, but they cannot fall right out of the pack and do not have to be replaced.

The cards are placed in a cradle, spindles are inserted as required and the cradle is then inverted so that the cards fall upside down. When the cradle is brought back to its normal position, the selected cards are upstanding and the name or other pertinent information is visible from the top of the rest of the pack.

In the second type, the features on the edge of the card are clipped. A rod is inserted in a jogger which vibrates the cards, causing those with desired characteristics to fall into place. Only those cards notched where the rod is situated will fall. If several rods are inserted in the jogger, only those cards notched in every position corresponding to the rod will fall. In this way it is possible to isolate cards with several characteristics in common.

The third type of card is purchased with a series of pre-punched holes on its edge. The holes, with the desired features, are slotted. A spindle is then inserted through the pack, in the desired hole, and lifted, isolating the cards with the perforations. The process is repeated with the remaining cards should a further division be required. Figure 7.13 shows an example of an edge-punched card.

	Item *A*	Item *B*	Item *C*
	Yes No	Yes No	Yes No
DO I WANT IT ? (if No, do not answer further questions) IS IT RELEVANT TO MY POSITION? (Do I need to have it to make better decisions?) DOES IT COME IN TIME ? DOES IT COME AT THE RIGHT FREQUENCY? (not more or less often than it should) IS IT ACCURATE ENOUGH? (not too inaccurate or unnecessarily accurate) IS ITS PRESENTATION IN THE BEST FORM FOR ME?			

Figure 1.1   Data appropriateness check list.
This checklist should be completed for each form that regularly crosses a desk in order to determine its appropriateness. The form can also be used to cover all written or statistical reports, minutes, carbons of letters, magazines and virtually anything found in the in-tray.

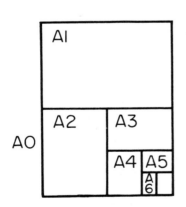
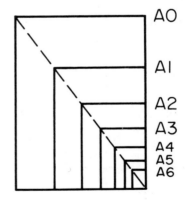

Figure 1.2   International paper sizes based on one square metre of trimmed paper.
The various sizes all have the same proportions.

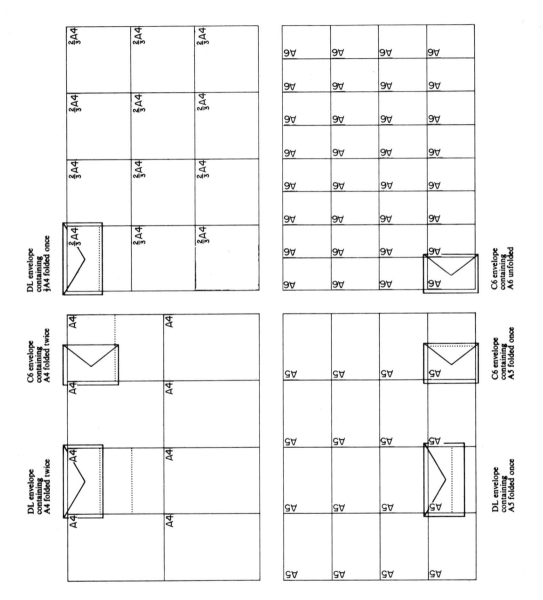

Figure 1.3   Metric size form plan showing how A4, two-thirds A4, A5 and A6 are cut economically from an A1 sheet of paper and how these examples fit well in the Post Office Preferred envelopes (Wiggins Teape Limited).

2

Records Required by Law

Every business has certain legal obligations to fulfill, particularly if there are employees, and these include the completion and maintenance of certain records. This information forms an integral part of a company's documentation and in fact may well form the basis of its information system.

An employer must, for example, maintain comprehensive records on earning of each employee and of tax and other deductions. He must also supply Government bodies such as the Ministry of Health and Social Security, the HM Inspector of Factories and Inland Revenue with certain information on employees.

Employers who intend to employ staff in an office or shop covered by the Offices, Shops and Railway Premises Act must complete HMSO Form OSR.1. A separate form must be completed for each set of premises with different postal address and two copies of each sent to HM Inspector of Factories for the district. The Act also requires a fire certificate to be in force with respect to each premises to which the Act applies where more than twenty persons are employed to work at any one time or where more than ten persons are employed elsewhere than on the ground floor. The employer has to apply to the fire authority for a fire certificate on Form OSR.3 obtainable from fire authorities or HM Inspector of Factories.

PAYE scheme

It is the employer's duty to deduct income tax from the pay of each employee according to the Government's Pay As You Earn (PAYE) scheme, which is simply a convenient method of collecting tax. Convenient, that is, for the Inland Revenue because it saves time collecting tax separately from each taxpayer. For the employer it means that he becomes, in effect, a tax collector with all the clerical work that entails.

An employer is obliged to report to the local Inland Revenue office any employee earning more than £8 a week and to deduct income tax from the employee's pay whether or not he has been directed to do so by the tax office. If he fails to do this he may be required to pay over to the Inland Revenue the tax which he should have deducted and, in addition, may incur liability to penalties.

Pensions to retired employees must also be taxed through PAYE. When normal employment ceases and the pension begins, the Inspector of Taxes should be notified and the subsequent returns should distinguish pensions from other earnings. However, a company may arrange for their pensions to be handled through an approved superannuation scheme so that both payment of the pension and deduction of the tax are taken out of the firm's hands.

Further details concerning the operation of the PAYE scheme are given in chapters 7 and 8.

National Insurance

An employer must also make payments for every employee to cover any employment tax, his contribution to the Redundancy Payment Fund and to cover all the different types of social insurance, such as unemployment, sickness and maternity benefits, pensions, and so on, under the National Insurance and the Industrial Injuries schemes. National Insurance contributions comprise two types of payment; a flat rate payment and a graduated payment. Each consists of an employer's contribution and the employee's share, which may be deducted from the employee's wages. In the first instance, however, it is the responsibility of the employer to make the whole of the payment to the Collector of Taxes with the income tax payments at the end of each income tax month. A National Insurance stamp of the appropriate value to the employee's flat rate contribution must be affixed to each employee's National Insurance card at the time the deduction is made (see page 156).

Employees who are members of an occupational pension scheme may be contracted out of the graduated contribution scheme if certain conditions are satisfied. The employer may then be issued with a certificate of non-participation issued by the Registrar of Non-Participating Employment, Penderel House, 287 High Holborn, London, WC1.

Contracts of employment

All employers are required under the Contracts of Employment Act of 1963 to issue a written statement of the basic terms and conditions of employment to all new employees within thirteen weeks of their engagement.

The Act does not require the contract itself to be in writing. What it does is to lay down certain minimum standards and require employers to give employees written information about the main terms of employment—pay, hours, holidays, and holiday pay, sickness and sickness pay, pensions and pension schemes and notice of termination of employment. The wording to be used in the statement is left to the discretion of each firm in accordance with its policy and practice. Each employee must be fully aware of his terms of engagement, understand what is expected of him, and know what he is entitled to by virtue of his employment.

The particulars to be included in the statement of terms of employment are:

1   Name and address of employer
2   Name and address of employee
3   Nature of employment
4   Date employment commenced
5   The scale or rate of remuneration or the method of calculating remuneration
6   The intervals at which remuneration is paid
7   Normal hours of work
8   Any terms or conditions relating to hours of work
9   Arrangements for overtime if worked
10 Terms and conditions relating to holidays and holiday pay
11 Terms and conditions relating to incapacity for work because of sickness or injury, including any provisions for sick pay and action to be taken by the employee
12 Pensions and pension schemes
13 Length of notice which the employee is obliged to give and is entitled to receive.

In each case where there are no particulars to be given the written statement must say so. For all or any of the particulars the written statement may refer the employee to a document or documents which he has reasonable opportunity of reading in the course of his employment, or which are made accessible to him in some other way. If all or any of the terms of employment are set out in a collective agreement, an employer may refer an employee to a copy of that agreement. Other documents which might be used in the same way are works handbooks, wages regulation orders, booklets about sick pay schemes or pension schemes, and notices about such things as work holidays.

If there is a change in the terms of employment the employer must inform the employees about it not more than a month after the change by means of a further written statement or by providing an up-to-date reference document. A notice of change on bulletin boards will be sufficient if the employee is advised in advance of this procedure.

Overtime reports

Employers must notify HM District Factory Inspector of their intention to employ women and young persons over sixteen on overtime. For this reason it is essential that whoever is responsible for notifying HM Factory Inspector be advised when young persons are to work overtime. In most cases a memo will suffice, although many firms have a specific form to ensure that all the information required is included.

Moreover, an employer is required by law to record all overtime worked by women and young persons in the prescribed Register so that control can be exercised in accordance with the Factories Act. If work is carried out in accordance with the 'individual overtime regulations' a card must be kept for each person indicating the number of hours and the number of days that the person has worked overtime. It is helpful if this card has a built-in reminder for the personnel manager when the maximum number of hours or weeks that may be worked in a year are approached.

General register

An employer whose premises fall under the definition of the Factories Act 1961 must keep a general register in the form prescribed by the Act. Among other things, the register must contain:

1   The prescribed particulars of the young persons employed in the factories.
2   The prescribed particulars of every accident and case of industrial disease occurring in the factory, of which notice is required to be sent to an inspector.
3   Particulars showing every exception under the Act of which the occupier of the factory avails himself—in the employment of male young persons in shifts in certain industries, for example.

The occupier of a factory must send HM Factory Inspector such extracts from the general register as the Inspector may from time to time require in the execution of his duties.

An employer intending to employ staff in an office or shop covered by the Offices, Shops and Railway Premises Act, must complete two copies of Form OSR.1 which should be sent to the HM Inspector of Factories for the district. A separate form should be completed for each set of premises with a different postal address.

Training records

An employer who wishes to qualify for a general grant from an industrial training board *must*, from the beginning of each year, maintain a training register of quantity and quality of training given and must produce up-to-date records for a training board's inspection as required. Training not supported in this way cannot be reported for grant claims.

Information on individual training can be integrated with other personal data on personal history records, although this may be impractical in larger firms or where considerable training is carried out. In this case it is wiser to maintain separate training records.

In general the training boards demand the following information for the training register:

1   Name of person being trained
2   Age, if under 21
3   Occupation for which he or she is being trained
4   Description of course being followed
5   Length and dates of course, giving number of days' training
6   Details of day and block release for further education where appropriate

The Knitting ITB further requires the trainee's National Insurance number, the registered number of the approved instructor, and starting date of employment.

It is also useful to indicate whether training is given on or off the job. If training is on the job the record should indicate whether the items recorded relate wholly to supernumerary training or whether the period consists of on-the-job experience, for example, or whether training contributed to production, because the board's assessors may wish to know this. The record can also include periods spent in off-the-job training at management courses, for example, or within the company, at discussions, talks and courses conducted by senior managers and specialists.

A syllabus of training is required by every training board for every individual listed on the register. In the case of employees on a formal training course, a code may be used to refer to the appropriate training programmes which should be kept available for inspection by the boards's assessors.

The boards also require all those involved with giving training to be enumerated. These may be categorised as:

1   Training officers
2   Instructors
3   Supervisory staff
4   Others: clerical staff employed in the training department, for example.

Work permits

Commonwealth citizens who take up or seek employment require a voucher by the Department of Employment. Applications for vouchers are placed in two categories. Category A applications are made by employers who have specific jobs to offer to a named Commonwealth citizen. Category B applications are made be Commonwealth citizens.

Commonwealth citizens already in the UK are normally in the same position as persons born in the UK when taking up, terminating or changing employment for which no special permit is required. An employer does not require a special permit to engage or terminate the employment of a Commonwealth citizen in this country.

An employer who wishes to employ a foreign worker must apply to the Department of Employment, Foreign Labour Division, Ebury Bridge House, Ebury Bridge Road, London SW1, for a permit. This permit is issued only for a particular job and for a particular person. The issue of a permit is subject to certain minimum requirements of age, skill and experience which vary according to the occupation and industry in which the alien is to be employed.

An exception is made for citizens of EEC countries. There is complete freedom of movement for workers in all EEC countries and no permit is required by employers in member countries to engage them.

Medical examinations

By law, no person under the age of eighteen may be taken into employment for more than fourteen days without a certificate of fitness from an appointed factory doctor. He may require a young person's school medical record from the local educational authority. In issuing a certificate of fitness the doctor has the power to specify an interval after which re-examination is necessary, and it is unlawful to retain the young person without re-examination and a renewal of the certificate. Any conditions imposed by the facory doctor in his certificate may continue to be enforced until the young person reaches the age of eighteen. When no shorter interval is specified, all employees under the age of eighteen are required by law to receive a medical examination at least once a year.

In addition, the factory doctor must make a report each year. The form of report required and the time at which the report is to be made is prescribed by the Appointed Factory Doctors Order.

In certain industries, *all* employees are required by law to be examined before starting work and then periodically. Also by law, all employers who normally employ more than thirty people are required to employ a quota of registered disabled persons as defined in the regulations of the Disabled Persons (Employment) General Regulations 1945.

Fire certificates

If more than twenty persons are employed to work at any one time or where more than ten persons are employed elsewhere than on the ground floor, the employer must apply for a fire certificate on Form OSR.3 obtainable from fire authorities or HM Inspector of Factories.

The application for a fire certificate is intended to satisfy fire authorities that the means of escape available in case of fire are adequate for the number of persons employed. The degree of risk in a set of premises within a building is related to the number of persons resorting there, including, for example, customers in a shop as well as the numbers employed there. Whenever possible the application should be accompanied by three copies of a plan of the building showing the proposed means of escape. For this purpose, copies of a simple sketch plan usually suffice.

The fire authorities must also be given notice of any proposed material alterations to the premises or change in the number of persons employed in any part of the premises which might effect the means of escape.

A fire certificate, once granted, must be kept on the premises to which it applies, and be readily available for inspection at any time.

Accident records

By law a record of any accident or 'dangerous occurrence' as defined by the Factories Act 1961, as well as industrial diseases, must be entered into the general register.

In addition, every employer who normally employs ten or more people in a factory is obliged to keep an accident book in which any injured employee may enter particulars of any accident which has happened to him at work. An accident book must be kept in every workroom so that it is readily accessible at all reasonable times. An entry in this book, if made as soon as practicable after the accident occurred, is sufficient notice of the accident to meet the requirements of the Industrial Injuries Act 1946.

Accident books should be retained permanently. Every employer must also by law report details of accidents to relevant Government ministries. Accidents causing loss of life or disabling a worker for more than three days from earning full wages at the work at which he was employed must be reported immediately to the District Inspector of Factories. Form F.43 must be used in all cases except where the accident or dangerous occurrence happens in the course of building operations or works of engineering construction. If an accident is fatal, the HM Factory Inspector must be informed immediately in writing. In premises covered by the Offices, Shops and Railway Premises Act, a different Form, OSR.2, must be used.

The Ministry of Social Security form relating to industrial injuries must also be completed if the employee claims that the accident happened at work.

Any industrial disease defined by the Notice of Industrial Diseases Order 1964 must be reported immediately to the District Inspector of Factories and to the appointed factory doctor.

In offices and other premises not covered by the Factories Act 1961 it is advisable for the employer to maintain a copy of Form OSR.2 so that a record of reportable accidents is maintained by the firm.

All employers are required by law, unless qualified for exemption under the Employers Liability (Compulsory Insurance Act), to insure against their liability for personal injury or disease sustained by their employers during the course of their work. In addition, employers are required to display a certificate confirming the contract of insurance at each of their premises or sites.

Public notices

The Factories Act requires that the following notices be displayed in every work room:

1   Hours and meal times

2   Any holidays substituted for statutory holidays
3   Address of HM Factory Inspector and Superintending Inspector
4   Name and address of factory doctor
5   The specific clock, if any, regulating the hours of work
6   The name of the person in charge of the first-aid box in every work room
7   The number of persons that can be employed in any work room
8   Prescribed abstract of the Act
9   Any special exceptions under sections 97—115 regarding factory hours which the company has been granted.

Other notices may be required to be displayed by the Dangerous or Welfare Orders which apply to specific industries and particular types of factories.

3

Principles of Bookkeeping

The best way to make sure a good business is not run into the ground is to keep proper accounting records. In the final analysis, whatever other records are kept, it is the financial data that enable management to make the necessary decisions for maintaining operations profitably and for planning developments. And of course financial statements are absolutely essential for substantiating allowances for tax purposes and for securing credit in any form.

Accounting principles are not something which have been laid down by Parliament. At best they are no more than an accumulation of well proven and well tested ideas. Every company is free to determine what records and bookkeeping procedures it feels are most suitable to its own peculiar circumstances.

The owner of a business will normally find it to his advantage to retain a trained public accountant to adapt an accountancy system to his special requirements. Public accountants render many other accounting services, incidentally, such as auditing, preparation of reports for government agencies, tax planning, and completion of tax returns and analyses of financial reports. A growing number of accountancy firms are also beginning to advise clients on a variety of specialised management services.

There are also many manufacturers of business equipment and business forms who will advise prospective customers on accounting procedures, though their advice will invariably lack objectivity. Computer service bureaux will also counsel prospective clients and many will accept responsibility for the whole of certain aspects of a company's accountancy records and prepare management reports as needed. A list of reputable computer bureaux, their services and their obligations as member firms, can be obtained from the Computer Services Bureaux Association, Leicester House, 8 Leicester Place, London WC2.

Basic bookkeeping records

Some sort of written record, however informal, should always be made at the time a transaction takes place. These may be nothing more than bits and pieces of paper—sales slips, credit memos, cash register tapes, written receipts, cheque counterfoils, petty cash slips, bank statements and so on. But these documents are important. They form the basis of any firm's bookkeeping system. The information from these various papers must be brought together in one or more journals or day books.

Function of journal or day book. A journal is simply a daily record of the transactions of the business in simple chronological order. Each journal entry shows:

1   Date of transaction
2   Brief description of transaction
3   Amount of money involved
4   Assets, liabilities, capital or type of income or expense affected by the transaction

Normally, journals are divided into two parts, one part for debits and the other for credits, that is, for money received and money paid. These should be on facing pages or side by side in their respective columns. This not only minimises bookkeeping procedures but streamlines the cash flow. Cash and credit sales or purchases should never be integrated, incidentally, but recorded in separate columns or separate pages in the journal and ledgers.

The example of the journal shown in Figure 3.1 has the additional summary section on the right for making daily totals and reconciling the books with the firm's bank statement.

As all business transactions are basically an exchange of one thing for another, double entry bookkeeping is often used to show this twofold effect by recording every transaction twice—as a debit entry in one account and as a credit entry in another. Either or both of the entries may be broken down into several items, but the total of the amounts entered as debits must be equal the total of the amounts entered as credits. At the end of each month a trial balance is taken, adding all debit balances and all credit balances to ensure that the two totals are the same before the individual items are too deeply buried.

Use of ledger accounts. To make the information recorded in the journal more usable, each item is later transferred, or *posted,* to a ledger account as a record of the increases, decreases and balance and for preparing financial statements.

A business uses as many different ledgers as it needs for keeping track of its operation. Many firms keep separate ledgers, for example, for recording sales and cash receipts, accounts receivable and accounts payable, employees' compensation, cash disbursements (purchases and expenses) and a general journal, sometimes called a journal 'proper' for recording assets, liabilities and capital, that is, all items having nothing to do with goods as such.

There is no reason, however, why smaller firms cannot make do with one simple ledger for recording all transactions, with separate pages or additional columns for isolating particular items as desired.

Balance sheets

At the end of each month and fiscal year a balance sheet is prepared summarising the company's assets, liabilities, and capital to show the condition of the business on a given date. Figure 3.3 is a typical example of a balance sheet.

A comparison of balance sheets will show changes although without any of the detail which would show how this was created. Such detail is obtained from the monthly and daily summaries described further on.

Profit and loss statements

The activities of the business during the period covered are summarised in a profit and loss statement which shows the income and expenses of the business during the period and the profit or loss that resulted. It is in effect a record of sales minus the cost of sales. In the final analysis it is this document which shows whether or not is is all worth the effort.

The frequency of profit and loss statements varies for different businesses, but ideally it should always be short enough to ensure adequate control of current operations. Some companies prepare them only quarterly and even annually, but this would seem inadvisable. A great deal can happen which can adversely affect a company within these periods. It would seem that monthly statements of trading activities are more relevant. Some campanies favour fortnightly or even weekly statements on the premise that remedial action can be taken more promptly on any variances that may be found. This is excellent, but only if such statements can be produced accurately and quickly without undue expense.

It is common practice to break down the items into standing charges (overhead expenses which must be met under any circumstances) and operating or running costs, which fluctuate according to business activity. Normally the operating costs are deducted from the revenue in the first instance to produce the operating income and the overhead expenses are then deducted to arrive at a profit or loss figure. Beside the actual trading figures are sometimes included cumulative figures for the year.

Figure 3.2 shows an example of a profit and loss statement. It should be stressed however that other subsections will invariably have to be included for different types of companies.

It is a good idea incidentally to calculate the ratio of net profit as a percentage of the sales. Any variation of the gross profit percentage between budget and actual will be directly reflected in the same variation between the budget and the actual results in the net profit. Therefore gross profit differences should be noted before starting to look for other reasons for variances in the net profit. For example:

	Forecast	Actual	Difference
	%	%	%
Gross profit	50	48.9	0.2
Net profit	10	8.9	1.2

However, a more satisfactory approach to ratios may be to take each type of expense as a percentage of sales and look at variations on their own merits and not as a relationship to net profit. This presumes that some expenses would be expected to vary according to the volume of sales but would rarely vary according to gross profit margin.
to the volume of sales but would rarely vary according to gross profit margin.

Budgeting procedures

In some companies a cash budget is prepared every month, forecasting, for example, the balance for the three months ahead, and is included on the profit and loss statement so that performance can be compared and measured each period. Normally the budget is prepared on the basis of receipts and payments and a monthly comparison is made between actual and estimated receipts and expenses.

Where no attempt is made to budget for future operations in any detail, the current progress of business against estimate should nevertheless be reviewed periodically.

Normally a budget is more effective when it includes the thinking of those who are to be guided by it and responsible for achieving its objectives rather than when it is solely the product of the owner/manager. This can be done by holding key persons in the organisation responsible for revenue and expense items under their direct control

In these circumstances it is important that budgeting procedures be well defined, to ensure that costs (and any revenue) are attributed consistently throughout the organisation. A summary of all departmental budgets should be made periodically on one sheet for easier analysis of the enterprise as a whole.

The accuracy of figures on departmental budgets is not crucial and time should not be spent unnecessarily in maintaining these books. Approximate figures are acceptable. What is more important is that excesses to the budgeted amounts be justified by the person responsible. On the other hand, there must be no spending spree at the end of the budget year for fear that future budgets will be reduced if the total allocation is not spent.

Figure 3.4 shows an example of a form used to compare actual expenditures and budgeted amounts for the administrative office.

Business summaries

A summary of sales and cash receipts should be made each day for proving cash in each till and for ultimate posting to the cash journal. Usually, total sales, collections on account and the total cash deposit are all entered on the same line of the journal, and the summary retained as a permanent record.

It is also useful to make weekly summaries of the same business transactions to facilitate the completion of the profit and loss statement. In many companies the balance sheet is also prepared from the summaries. This saves a little time, but it does leave the other accounts open to some doubt because, while a balance sheet would prove they were basically correct, it would not necessarily prove them to be correct in detail.

Figures 3.5 and 3.6 show examples of a daily and a weekly businesss summary.

Payment records

Every payment should have some sort of written document to support it—an invoicee, petty cash voucher, payroll summary and so on. If such support is not available for some good reason, a memo stating what the payment is for should be prepared for approval by an authorised person.

Invoices should be checked in some way to ensure that the goods or services have in fact been received and that the terms and amount are correct. Invoices should be reconciled with goods received note or purchase order, for instance. Often the order number and the goods received note are written on the invoice as a check that this matching has been done. The arithmetic (extensions, additions and discounts) on large invoices should aslo be checked to make sure that no errors have been made in computing. Sample checks suffice for small value invoices.

Invoices should be marked Paid and the date and cheque number shown to prevent their being paid a second time. Supporting documents should be filed in a paid-bills file in alphabetical order by payee.

If payments are made by cheque the couterfoils can be used for posting in the ledger. The chequebook counterfoil will provide enough data to determine in some detail just how the money is being spent and also serves as a receipt.

Payments through credit transfers are a relatively cheap and simple method for making payment. The firm's bank is provided with Giro slips and a Giro schedule listing each creditor's name and amount and signed by a senior director or manager of the company. In this way only one cheque needs to be completed. In some systems a suitable authority to cover payment is incorporated into the schedule, obviating the need to write a cheque.

Auditors may insist that a copy of the Giro schedule be stamped by the bank and retained for auditing purposes. This is easily done by either making an additional carbon copy of the schedule or by taking the cash journal or ledger page to the bank for stamping.

Petty cash slips

To avoid having to write many cheques for small purchases, it is wise to keep a petty cash fund from which to make small payments. Each time a payment is made a petty cash slip (available from most stationery shops) is made out stating the amount paid and the purpose. If an invoice or a receipt is available it should be attached to the petty cash slip for filing.

The slips should be kept with the petty cash. At all times the total of the amounts recorded and the sum remaining in the fund should total the original amount of the fund. When the total of the petty cash slips approaches the fixed float, a cheque is made out to Petty Cash for the amount of the slips, and the amount simply debited to petty cash in the journal.

In most firms a maximum is set on the amount to be spent from petty cash and any amount over the specified sum must be approved by an immediate supervisor.

In retail outlets, the same fund is sometimes used to serve for both petty cash and change, and the petty cash slips are used to balance the day's transactions.

Petty cash slips should be cancelled or marded in such a way as to prevent their re-use. A good way to handle these is to summarise them on the outside of an envelope, showing the date, cheque number and the amount of the cheque used to restore the fund and file the slips in the envelope.

Regular analyses should be made of petty cash purchases to see if any items are being pucrchased in sufficient quantity in local shops to make it worthwhile to stock them. Figure 3.7 shows a specimen petty cash expenditure form.

Accounts payable ledger

All unpaid bills can be filed together and a list prepared at the end of each month, showing the suppliers, the amount owed to each and the total. Where no price is given, an estimate of the price should be made. If most of the suppliers are the same each month, the list can be typed on multi-column paper and a separate column used for each month. This has two advantages over a separate listing for each month. It saves rewriting most of the suppliers's names and it gives a month-to-month comparison of accounts payable.

The total of the accounts payable should be entered in the cash disbursements journal in the month in which they were made (whether or not they have been paid for) for tax purposes. When payment is made, it is recorded as any other payment.

Handling cash receipts

Cash receipts in hand should be balanced each day with the sales receipts when doing the daily business summary. Receipts should be issued in strict numerical sequence and a record kept of those to whom they are issued. Continuous stationery helps to ensure that receipts are kept together. There are on the market registers designed to produce handwritten sales slips with carbon copies which are automatically filed in numerical sequence in a locked compartment.

A comparison between the receipt counterfoil or duplicates and the entries of the daily summaries should be made from time to time without notice and all receipts accounted for. Great care should also be used over the security of books of unused receipts. Shortages should be investigated without delay and in serious cases, all relevant documents, receipt counterfoils and books should be removed from the possession of interested parties.

Holding large sums of money overnight and particularly at weekends should be avoided. This can be achieved by calculating the money required each day so that only the minimum float is kept and the remainder deposited.

Cheques given in payment of purchases should be examined to verify the date and the name of the payee and to ensure that they have been properly signed. The figures and the written amount should agree. All cheques and any other money orders received as payment should be compared with the original invoice or statement and any discrepancy noted.

Acceptable cheques should then be stamped with the company's name and separated from the accompanying documents. The amount on the cheques and on the documents should be separately totalled, preferably with an adding machine, to make sure that the respective totals agree.

It is difficult, incidentally, to understand why shops and even banks often ask customers to write their address on the back of a cheque. This suggests somehow that while one may forge a name one would never give a false address. The customer should be asked for some form of identification with his address and the address written on the cheque by the clerk.

Accounts receivable ledger

The simplest method of handling credit accounts—other than just keeping a file of sales slips—is to have an accounts receivable ledger with a separate sheet for each customer to record all purchases, payments and returns. If the number of accounts is considerable it may be more feasible to record all transactions on separate ledger cards. Figure 3.8 shows a very simple and basic ledger card for recording both debits and credits which can be used for either sales of purchase credit accounts.

After the daily summary of business has been completed, the charge sales checks and cash receipts slips for payments on account should be arranged in alphabetical order and posted to the individual customers' accounts in the ledger. Each entry should show the date, the sales check number and the amount of the sale, which is recorded in the debit column. When the day's posting has been completed, the sales checks should be filed by dates.

If the business has a number of credit transactions, bookkeeping time can be saved by accumulating each customer's sales slips and receipts in a folder or pocket during the month instead of posting each one separately in the ledger. At the end of the month, the sales slips can be added and the adding machine tape or a pencilled addition stapled to them and endorsed with a statement showing only the customer's balance at the end of the month. The one total is then entered on the customer's ledger sheet.

In addition to the individual customer accounts, a control sheet should be set up and the total charges and receipts entered from the daily summary. At any time, the balance on the control sheet should equal the total of the balances of all the individual accounts. If the accounts receivable ledger balances without difficulty each month, it may be possible to do away with the control sheet and balance the accounts directly to the accounts receivable ledger.

Monthly statements

At the end of each month a statement is normally sent to each customer listing all the various invoices, debit notes, credit notes and receipts which have been sent to the customer during that period. Before the statements are put in the envelopes for mailing, however, the ending balances shown on all statements should be totalled to make sure that the total agrees with the balance shown on the accounts receivable control sheet. This can take the place of the end-of-the-month balancing of the account receivable ledger. It will check, not only the accuracy of the ledger, but also the accuracy of the statements.

Many firms now simply use the term *To account rendered* .... on the statement and only state the outstanding amount, thus saving the trouble of listing all the entries and calculations for each customer at the end of the month.

Mechanised bookkeeping systems used in many companies now enable entries to be typed on the customer's statement at the same time as they are made on the accounts. The statement in effect becomes a copy of the customer's ledger card for that month, with the beginning balance, sales, returns, cash payments and ending balance. The statement is therefore ready to be sent out at the end of the month with no extra work.

Credit control

Customers having long overdue balances should be noted as statements are prepared each month, and a reminder of the unpaid balance enclosed with the statement to these customers.

There is no question that credit stimulates sales, but many firms, particularly small businesses eager to sell and more eager to please, can be all too generous in trying to attract new custom and let credit run up to dangerous levels. The businessman may find it necessary to get extra finance to see him through. Credit control must be rigidly applied, no matter what size the customer or his orders if the firm is to survive financially.

It is accepted that few customers pay until asked and it is also a fact that the older the debt the less the chance of payment. The customer must therefore not only be reminded but made constantly aware of the existence of a rigid control system which will readily bring to light delinquent accounts which are kept outstanding until remedial action has been taken.

Normally a series of routine letters requesting payments, each more strongly worded, is sent out at regular intervals. It is unwise, incidentally, to have such letters signed by the owner or senior manager of the firm as this may result in personal ill will.

Ledger cards or sheets should be coded to indicate delinquent payers and should state any credit limits. At least twice a year a schedule should be prepared showing open accounts and the amounts that are current, those that are 60 to 90 days old and so on. Such reviews assist greatly in setting up bad debt reserves and in checking credit and collection practices.

Multi-posting systems

There are available commercially a number of multi-posting systems by which credit sales can be recorded in a sales day book, the customer's individual ledger card, and the monthly statement at one writing. In this case the loose leaf journal sheet is placed first on the register or collator with the appropriate statement and ledger card on top. A posting is then made on the statement and the impression is reproduced on the ledger card and journal sheet. When a run of postings has been completed it is proved and balanced immediately. As all three records are completed together during the month, statements are always up to date and ready for mailing as soon as the month's postings are completed; the lengthy business of month-end balancing is eliminated. Daily runs of postings should be proved on the adding machine however to ensure the accuracy of each statement.

In the same way, purchases can be recorded on a supplier's ledger card and purchase journal sheet and on a remittance advice note.

Figures 3.9 and 3.10 show examples of documents designed for completing entries at one writing. The second illustration, Figure 3.10, is particularly interesting because each one of the documents has been designed for manifold purposes. The ledger sheet for example, can be used as a sales, purchase, cash or general day book with a complementary ledger card which can be used either as a customer's or supplier's account. The statement may also be used as either a statement or remittance advice. In this way stock holdings of forms are reduced and there is no difficulty in re-ordering forms.

The multi-posting system can also be used to complete bank giro slips. The entry on each slip is carbon copied on to a cash book sheet which contains the details of the bank and branch. The sheet also contains columns for discounts and totals so that the books can be balanced (see Figure 3.11).

OFFICE ACCOUNT CASH BOOK

Sheet number _____

Date	Detail	Reference	Payments		Receipts		Ledger account balance	Summary cash account				Ledger account old balance		Ledger account
								Total received		Total paid				

Figure 3.1   Cash book (George Anson Limited).

PROFIT AND LOSS STATEMENT

Period number _____   Week(s) ending

                                        This period   Year to date

Sales   _____   _____

Credit sales   _____   _____

less Materials   _____

      Wages   _____

      Total variances   _____

      Standard cost of sales _____

Gross profit   _____   _____

less Rent   _____

      Rates   _____

      Transport   _____

      Administration   _____

      Loan interest   _____

      Bank interest   _____

Other income   _____   _____

Net profit   _____   _____

Figure 3.2   Profit and loss statement.

BALANCE SHEET

_____19

Fixed assets
Land _____
Buildings _____
Delivery equipment _____
Furniture and fixtures _____ £_____
    Less allowance for depreciation
                                          £_____

Leasehold improvements, less amortisation _____
Total fixed assets _____

Current assets
Cash:
    Cash in bank £_____
    Petty cash _____ £_____
Accounts receivable £_____
    Less allowance for doubtful accounts _____ _____
Goods inventories _____
    Total current assets £_____
Total assets £_____

Capital:
    Proprietor's capital, beginning of period £_____
    Net profit for the period £_____
    Less proprietor's drawings _____
    Increase in capital _____
    Capital, end of period £_____
Long-term liabilities
    Note payable, due after 1 year _____
Current liabilities
    Accounts payable _____
    Notes payable, due within 1 year _____
    Payroll taxes and withheld taxes _____
    Sales taxes _____
        Total current liabilities _____
Total liabilities £_____
Total liabilities and capital £_____

Figure 3.3   Balance sheet.
If the business suffers a loss, the proprietor's drawings are *added* to the net loss to give the total *decrease* in capital.

Administration budget : Month of						
Expenses	Actual	Budget	Var	Cumulative Actual	Budget	Var ±
Salaries						
Wages						
Nat Ins, Graduated pension						
Electricity						
Heating						
Rent/rates						
Water						
Printing/stationery						
Postage						
Telephones						
Office furniture and equipment						
Training levy						
Expenses						
Transport/travelling						
Training courses conferences						
Repairs & maintenance, offices						
Totals						

Figure 3.4   Administration budget.

DAILY SUMMARY OF BUSINESS	Till A		Till B		Total	
Cash sales						
Vending machines						
Cigarettes cash						
Telephone calls						
Money found						
Total cash takings						
Overs +						
Shorts −						
Total cash takings net						
Credit accounts						
Total turnover						
Petty cash						
Post						
Travel						
Stationery						
Plant sundries						
Cleaning materials						
Laundry						
Petty cash total						
Purchases						
Wages vouchers						
Float increase						
Total expenditure (1)						
Banking (2)						
Reconciliation (1 + 2)						
ANALYSIS OF TURNOVER						
Product category X						
Product category Y						
Product category Z						
Spare parts						
Repairs						
Total turnover						
Wage packets in safe						
Float retained						

Date_____

Authorised signature_____

Figure 3.5   Daily summary of business.

WEEKLY SUMMARY OF BUSINESS		
Cash sales		
Vending machines		
Cigarettes cash		
Telephone calls		
Money found		
Total cash takings		
Over +		
Shorts −		
Total cash takings net		
Credit accounts		
Total turnover		
Petty cash		
Post		
Travel		
Stationery		
Plant sundries		
Cleaning materials		
Laundry		
Total petty cash		
Purchases		
Wage vouchers		
Float increases		
Total expenditure		
Banking		
Reconciliation		
Product X		
Product Y		
Product Z		
Spare parts		
Repairs		
Total turnover		
Wage packets in safe		
Float retained		
	Authorised signature _____	

Figure 3.6   Weekly summary of business.

PETTY CASH EXPENDITURE														
Brief details if no bill attached	Post		Travel		Stationery		Plant sundries		Cleaning materials		Laundry		Total		Signature
Totals															

Figure 3.7   Petty cash expenditure form.

Account number		Name				Date	Item	Reference	Debit	Credit	Balance
Date	Item	Reference	Debit	Credit	Balance						

Account number		Name				Date	Item	Reference	Debit	Credit	Balance
Date	Item	Reference	Debit	Credit	Balance						

Address			Telephone number		Credit limit	

	Account number	Name	Account outstanding since												
			Jan	Feb	Mar	April	May	June	July	Aug	Sept	Oct	Nov	Dec	

Figuree 3.8   Ledger card.
A visible edge sheet has been inserted for credit control purposes. The tab on the left indicates that no further credit may be extended (Remington Rand).

LEDGER SHEET

Date	Reference	Details	Debit		Credit		Balance		Account number	Old balance		Name
Nov 15	862	Goods	27	04			220	85	194	193	81	H. George Ltd.
Nov 15	48	Goods	56	72			175	16	229	118	44	Jonson & Sons
										50	75	B.H. Wire & Co
										105	00	Carry Transport
										170	64	Adus Mfg
										30	15	Pilgrim & Co
										45	17	R.B. White Ltd.
										221	33	J. Click Ltd.
									37	165	52	H. Diment Ltd.
									37	75	06	Chas Fair Ltd.
									37	60	16	Fox Furriers
									37	24	22	C. Lowe & Co
									37	90	95	N. Sedge Ltd
									37	125	60	Charles & Owen
									37	150	26	P Lawson
									37	80	10	R.B. Brown
									37	29	41	Rima Co Ltd
									37	60	02	L. Morris Ltd.
									37	102	47	Gox & Co
									37	140	00	T. Price Ltd
									37	52	55	Sandwell Co
									37	110	18	W. Hall
									37	91	15	S. Burns & Son

Name: G. BURNS & SONS Account number 37

Address: 40 WORKS ROAD Card number 2

HERONGATE Terms NET

Date	Reference	Details	Debit		Credit		Balance		Account number
Sep 2	42	Goods	14	07			124	95	37

STATEMENT

G. Burns & Sons
40 Works road,
Herongate.

Date	Reference	Details	Debit		Credit		Balance	
Nov 1		To account rendered						
Nov 3	762	Goods	93	15			93	15
" 4	781	Goods	4	10			97	25
" 8	34	Returns			6	10	91	15
" 15	57	Goods	5	04			96	19

Figure 3.9 Documents used for multi-posting credit accounts.
The ledger card is printed on both sides, accommodating a total of 44 entries (Lamson Paragon Limited).

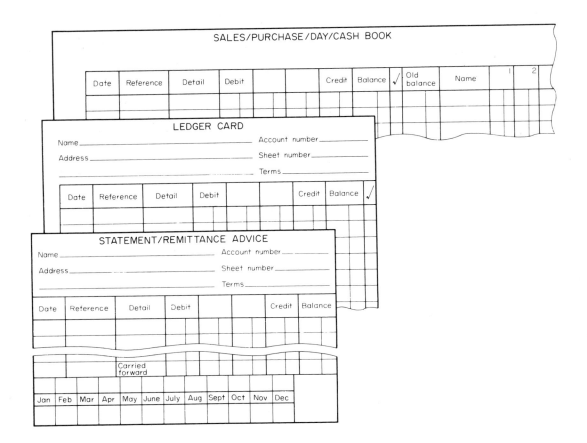

Figure 3.10   Documents designed for use in multi-posting.
The ledger sheet contains 22 columns and the number of the sheet is inset so that it can be guillotined if fewer columns are needed. On the ledger side, there are two debit columns and two credit columns. The second debit column and the first credit column are not headed so that the two can be placed together. Alternatively the blank column can be used for recording purchase tax, discounts or cash returns. At the bottom of the ledger card is a provision for ageing balance with a section for each month of the year (George Anson Limited).

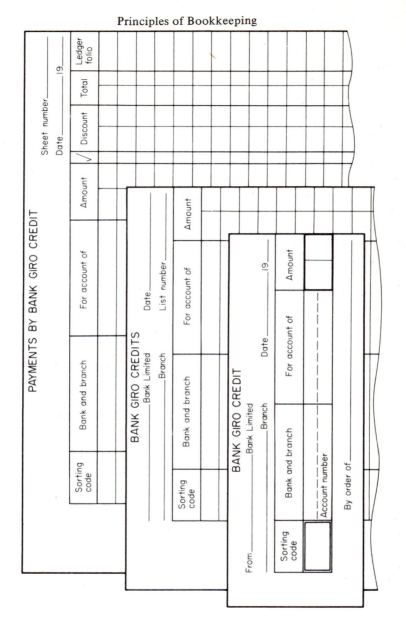

Figure 3.11 Multi-posting system for payments by Giro (George Anson Limited).

4

Recording and Control of Purchases

Careful control of purchases is essential for maintaining optimum stock—neither too much nor too little of any line to meet production requirements and sales demand. Shortages of even one item can cause serious losses and create delays in meeting production schedules and fulfilling orders.

At the same time it is important to determine the right *economical order quantity*—how much to order at any one time to obtain the best prices without creating excess stock. For many companies, cash discounts through bulk buying can be greater than the net profits on certain items but an over enthusiasm to take advantage of such discounts can lead to surplus stock and can make a serious dent in the company profits. Excess stock is waste of both money and valuable space. There is, moreover, the additional risk of damage, soiling, and the danger that long-held stock may become absolete. Surplus stock is in fact considered one of the major causes of business failure.

Determining the economical order quantity

There are various sophisticated mathematic formulae for calculating the economical order quantity.

Essentially, the EOQ for any item depends on the following factors:

1   Minimum order accepted by the supplier
2   Difference in price for various quantities
3   Quantity to be used within a stated period of time, based on sale and production and sales forecasts
4   Value of the item
5   Difficulty in obtaining the item

6   Transportation and storage costs
7   Special problems, such as the danger of spontaneous combustion with
      certain items
8   Procurement cost an order.

Not all of this information will be available from a central reference point or recorded
on any single document. But once determined, the EOQ should be recorded for each
item and kept up-to-date as circumstances change.

Form of purchase order

A purchase order is the company's authorised document for purchasing goods. Figures
4.1 and 4.2 show two typical examples of purchase orders. In most firms the purchase
order is the principal, and very often, the only authority for accepting goods from a
supplier. Telephone orders for urgent goods are invariably followed with a formal
document. Insistence that all orders are written on the firm's order forms ensures that a
complete and clear statement exists of the various conditions agreed upon.

   A purchase order is a contract and subject to legal enforcement, although
agreements by word or mouth, telephone, telegram, telex or any other written note,
can all be equally binding in law. It is therefore important that any order be accurate.

Format.   Efforts have been made to design a standard order form to assist suppliers
and reduce the huge range of shapes, sizes, colours, layouts and contents. The British
Standards Institution has recommended the layout shown in Figure 4.3 but no actual
form has been found to conform to this layout.

   Almost everyone seems to put the supplier's name and address at the upper left side,
for instance, although there is good reason for putting it at the upper right hand side as
recommended by the BSI. If the order form is filed in some way which entails fastening
it at the left, the two key references for locating a particular order should really be at
the right where they are most readily seen. These key references are the supplier's name
and the order number.

Contents.   In general the purchase order forms should include provisions for the
following:

1   The instructions *Please supply* or *Please supply the undermentioned* above
      the part of the order which details requirements
2   Supplier's name and address
3   Name and address of purchasing organisation with telephone number and
      telex code if there is one
4   Date of order

5   Description of what is required
6   Quantity required
7   Delivery date
8   Delivery address if different from item 2. If these two items are the same, instructions should read *Please supply at our address given below*
9   Price and discount
10   Terms of payment
11   Order number.

In addition a purchase order form may include any of the following:

12   Signature
13   Special instructions for packaging
14   Special instructions for invoicing
15   Internal references, such as requisition number, stock number, job or contract number
16   Special transport arrangements
17   Special inspection arrangements
18   Supplier's reference, such as quotation number
19   Provision for acknowledgement of order (by extra copy or tear off coupon, for example)
20   Any special or general terms and conditions of purchase, including quality of the materials and workmanship, both of which may be subject to the approval of the buyer.

Numbering.   Every order should have a reference number, and suppliers should be required to state this number on all invoices and other documents. Accounting for numbered order forms gives close control of all purchase commitments and it useful for keeping track of and reconciling various copies.

Sets of order forms are usually numbered consecutively in printing. Alpha prefixes or suffixes are sometimes used to key the order to the employee or department who has requisitioned the goods or to particular jobs. Some firms prefer to type the number of each order as it is prepared because more than one person may have a set of purchase orders. This makes it easier to account for each order issued but requires that some sort of register be kept. On the other hand, each order number can be made to signify the category of the purchase, the type of product, work project on which the goods are to be used, the date of issue or any other classification which may be related to bookkeeping records.

Acknowledgement forms.   Some firms provide at the foot of the order form an acknowledgement slip perforated so that it can be detached and returned to the buyer to confirm the order (see Figure 4.4). Alternatively, two copies of the order, one of them marked *Acknowledgement* can be sent to the supplier with a request that it be signed and returned. Acknowledgements are normally filed with the order, separately by order number or by suppliers name. It should be pointed out, however, that many acknowledgements are not returned and their use rarely justifies the time and cost involved in chasing them.

Copies.   At least two copies of each order are necessary, one for the supplier and another to be retained by the buyer as a record of orders placed and a check against their completion. Additional copies may be made for any of the following:

1   Stores—to update stock control records
2   Warehouse—as an advice of goods or materials to be received and their expected delivery date. Necessary arrangements can then be made for their arrival and storage.
3   Accounts—to write off against the budget
4   For progressing orders

Sets of purchase orders and the use of copies to serve other purposes are described in greater detail in the following chapters.

Filing purchase orders

In most firms the file copy of the order is withdrawn as soon as completed, leaving only the outstanding orders in the active file. In this way the full index consists only of live records, some of which may require attention.

Completed orders should be filed in the method easiest for reference. If orders are most often referred to by supplier, they should be filed alphabetically according to the supplier's name. If the firm is concerned with only a few large projects the order could be filed alphatically under each project.

Once placed, orders should not be amended but should be marked *cancelled* or *voided* and filed just as if they had been completed. A new order should then be made out and sent to the supplier with a covering letter clearly marked *Purchase Order Amendment.*

Progressing orders

Outstanding orders left in the active file should be checked monthly or weekly on a routine basis to identify those requiring attention.

Some firms write each order in a binder with the supplier's name and due date beside it and cross through the entry when the order is completed. It sometimes proves difficult to find those orders which need urging among all those crossed out, however, particularly where there is a large volume of orders. A simpler way is to enter each order in a large desk diary under the date due for progressing, which could be two or three weeks before the date due for delivery if the goods are crucial to production. If order number 1004 is to be followed on 11 November, for instance, it would be written in under that date in the diary. Alternatively, details of orders can be typed on a card for each day of the year instead of being handwritten in a diary. In smaller firms it may only be necessary to record orders on separate sheets of paper for each month of the year.

All of these methods involve additional recording and clerical work and, in some circumstances, it is simpler to code each order with a coloured tab to indicate when the order needs attention. The orders remain filed alphabetically according to supplier or numerically by order number. On the other hand, the orders can be filed in chronological order by due date, but this approach makes retrieval difficult in all but the smallest firms.

If many orders need to be progressed, it may be feasible to make an extra copy of the order form specifically for use in progressing. The copies can be filed in folders made out for each month of the year. A small firm may have only four folders: due this month, due next month, due in three months, and due later this year. In large firms, the first folders can be numbered 1 to 31 for the days of the current month, and the next twelve labelled from January to December for the other months of the year. A few additional files can also be provided for subsequent years. Any correspondence regarding orders may also be held in these progress folders.

Action taken on any order should be noted along with the date, and the order form or progress copy should be designed to provide space for this purpose, either at the bottom or on the reverse side of the form (see Figure 4.5). Changes in expected delivery date should also be entered, showing amendment number, and the form re-filed accordingly. Any diary entry should be amended and the originator of the requisition notified, unless it is understood that the delivery date is not crucial.

Before proceeding to chase an order, however, it may be wise to make sure that the goods ordered have not in fact been delivered. A list of goods received could be prepared by the stockroom on a daily basis. If Goods Received department are given a copy of each order a quick check can be made of their records of outstanding orders.

Purchase requisitions

The purposes of purchase requisition are threefold:

1   To notify the buyer that something is required
2   To authorise the expenditure of company funds to buy it
3   To record who asked for what, at what time and for when, who gave the go-ahead and what was done about it

Many purchase requisition forms are too complicated for the job they do. The form should request just the information it needs and in the same sequence in which it will be subsequently copied on to inquiry or order forms. This could include any of the following:

1   Requisition number
2   Date of requisition
3   Description of the goods required
4   Quantity
5   Date required
6   Stock number
7   Number used in last three months
8   Delivery instruction
9   Any other special instructions
10 Originator of the requisition
11 Authorisation
12 Department or accountancy code number
13 Job or contract number
14 Suggested supplier

Figure 4.6 is a typical example of a purchase requisition. It is common practice for a requisition to be completed in duplicate, one part being retained by the originator until the goods are received. In some firms the requisitions are used for progressing purposes. The supplier's name and order number are entered on the requisition form and the orders can then be filed away to await invoice.

The requisition can itself serve as the purchase order. Figure 4.7 shows an example of such a form. Two copies go directly to the supplier, one copy is returned to stores, and one is kept by the buyer. The supplier keeps one copy as proof of order and sends the other with the goods to serve as an advice note and goods received note. When the goods come in, this copy is married up by the storesman with the copy which was sent to him at the time the order was placed. The stock control records are updated and the signed copy is sent to the office to await invoice.

Travelling requisition

The travelling requisition, also called permanent order cards, contains all the permanent data necessary for ordering a standard stock item. This would include, for example, the item classification, code number, description, and so on, as well as other relevant data such as consumption rates, approved suppliers and any contracts applicable.

When the re-order point is reached (see page 67) the travelling requisition is raised, the required re-order quantity and delivery date inserted and the order approved by an authorised person. The supplier's name, order number and date promises are then entered on the record by the buyer. The card is kept outstanding until the goods are received, when it is routed back to the stockroom or, if the item is required by only one department, to the originator.

The travelling requisition can be incorporated in the stock record or serve as a purchasing record as well as a requisition. It can, for example, include a purchase history of the item which may eliminate the need for separate purchase history records.

While there is much to be said in favour of the travelling requisition, it cannot be used in all cases. But where it can, this simple record is a great time saver for repeat orders. It can be used for years without re-typing of data. As there is no need to complete details for each order, time is saved in dispatching of orders and there is no possibility of errors creeping in. And, because the terminology is standardised, there is no confusion on the item requisitioned and ordered.

Figures 4.8 and 4.9 are examples of travelling requisitions.

Index of suppliers

At the very least the buyer should have a simple alphabetical list with the name, address and telephone number of each regular supplier and possibly the names of personal contacts.

It is usually best to concentrate purchases with a relatively small number of suppliers, rather than to spread them widely. This helps to reduce the amount of forms and paperwork involved in purchasing, with fewer accounts to control on the bought ledger, and should result in better service and purchasing terms.

For this reason it is useful to include on each supplier's card the type of equipment which can be supplied. If the range of goods purchased is limited this can be done by means of various coloured tabs. Alternatively, it may be better to keep a separate index of suppliers cross referenced either by part number or type of material.

The time spent in getting together such an index will be saved elsewhere. One company informs every calling representative that, having seen them once, their name, company products will be recorded and the company would in future see them only when required. The company is kept informed of any new product or company development by post and telephone.

Purchase history records

It is useful to record the history of purchases with each supplier and to make a seasonal study of the volume sold of each vendor's goods, including some measure of their productivity. Such records have value when fixing contract terms. If reciprocal trading has been agreed the total amount of purchases should be compared with sales to the supplying company monthly or quarterly. Purchase history records should show what quantities have been purchased, how much was paid and the date. Such records can also be used to record the supplier's performance concerning delivery, quality of goods and after-sales service. Comments need not be only adverse; many suppliers go out of their way to help customers and this should not be forgotten when placing new orders.

Figure 4.10 shows a typical example of a supplier record.

It may be preferable to record purchases on separate cards for each individual item. This pinpoints the various suppliers used at various times, the different prices paid and so on. The choice of system depends very much on the type and size of industry and the amount of purchasing. Sometimes both systems are useful. Figures 4.11 and 4.12 are good examples of this type of record. The purchase history form illustrated in Figure 4.13 was designed to serve as the progressing document. After details of the order are recorded, the order is filed and the progress date is signalled on the visible edge.

It is not necessary to keep records on every item or every supplier, however. It is sufficient to concentrate on regular suppliers and the more major items. The volume of requirements, the value of the purchase, how critical the items are to company operations or product functioning, the level of quality required, how regularly the item is purchased—these are some of the factors to consider in deciding whether or not to maintain comprehensive records.

If is is not practical to make a vendor analysis, each vendor should be asked to report his total sales to the firm each season. Inventory can then be taken by vendor lines. The comparison of sales with closing and opening inventories gives a reasonably accurate measure of the relative value of the different sources.

Function and form of quotation requests

It may appear to be a good idea to check the market occasionally, though in general it is not particularly good business to switch suppliers constantly without very good reason. In a few instances where there is no regular source for an item, or where it has not been ordered for some time, it may be feasible to obtain quotations from several suppliers. It should not be necessary to have special quotation form. Such requests can be made on an ordinary letterhead. If they are frequently made, however, it is helpful to have a preprinted form letter to which details of the goods required may be attached (see Figure 4.14). The requisition form can perhaps be designed so that it can be duplicated and the copy attached to the covering letter to serve as the enquiry form. Enquiry forms can include any of the following:

1 The words *Enquiry* or *Request for quotation* boldly stated at the top to avoid any misunderstanding.
2 Name and address of purchasing organisation with phone number and telex code where appropriate
3 Date
4 Description of what is required and purpose if not evident
5 Quantity required
6 Date required or period covered, where appropriate
7 Place of delivery
8 Special conditions applicable to this particular transaction

9 Terms of payment
10 Reference number

A formal letter confirming details on the enquiry form can be considered as an order.

Handling small purchases

Small orders can be costly to process and can take up a lot of time which should be devoted to more expensive and more important purchases. There are several procedures in addition to the use of petty cash for processing orders with the minimum of paperwork and as quickly as possible.

Standing orders can be placed for regular deliveries according to requirements, with invoices submitted on a monthly basis.

Blanket orders can be placed with suppliers against which orders can be called off as required by authorised persons without the need to initiate a separate order form. Sometimes the supplier will agree to hold specified minimum quantities permanently in stock, thus reducing in some small way the stockholding of the company itself.

At least one company in the UK encloses a crossed cheque with the order form for small purchases thus cutting out invoices altogether. If the price is unknown, a blank cheque is enclosed. This approach has saved clerical work, forms, envelopes, improved relations with the suppliers—for one thing, they're getting immediate payment—and enables the firm to earn more in cash discounts as an extra bonus. A limit is usually stated on the cheque and a spot check is carried out regularly to identify any dishonest suppliers, but so far there have been no discrepancies.

This is rather an adventurous approach, however, and most firms prefer to follow the more traditional methods, the more popular of which are the standing and blanket orders and petty cash systems.

PURCHASE ORDER

To _____

Address _____

_____   Date of order _____

Deliver to _____   Delivery date _____

Please supply

Special instructions

Signed _____

Please notify us immediately if you are unable to deliver by the date required

Figure 4.1   Purchase order form.
A standard continuous form for use on a Paragon register (Lamson Paragon).

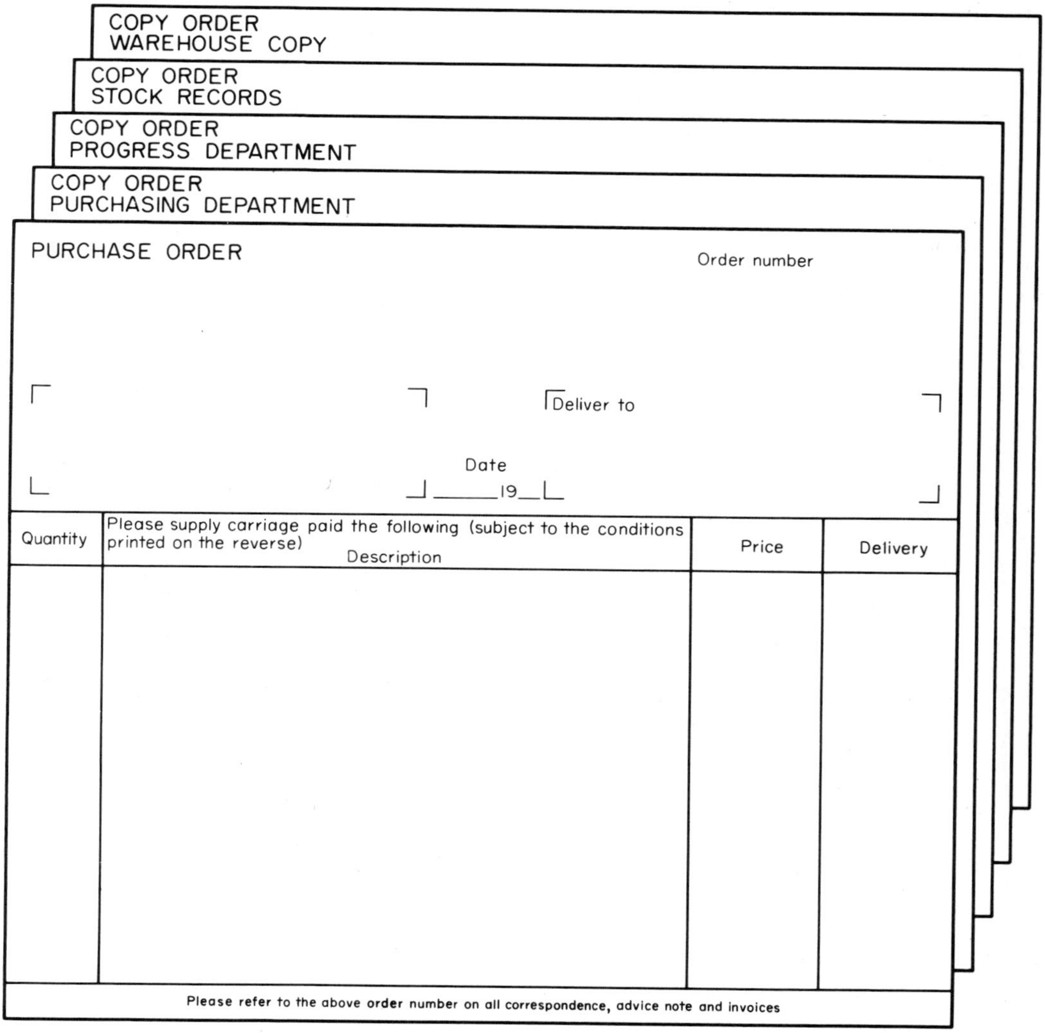

COPY ORDER
WAREHOUSE COPY

COPY ORDER
STOCK RECORDS

COPY ORDER
PROGRESS DEPARTMENT

COPY ORDER
PURCHASING DEPARTMENT

PURCHASE ORDER   Order number

⌐   ¬   ⌐Deliver to   ¬

                              Date
└   ┘ ____19__└   ┘

Quantity	Please supply carriage paid the following (subject to the conditions printed on the reverse) Description	Price	Delivery

Please refer to the above order number on all correspondence, advice note and invoices

Figure 4.2 Purchase order.
This company uses Lamson Paragon Speedisets for making four additional copies of each order for internal distribution at one typing. Conditions of purchase are printed on the reverse side of the top copy, which is sent to the supplier. Part 2 is the company's record of the order and a check against completion. Part 3 is used for progressing and Part 4 for updating stock records. Part 5 is passed to the warehouse as an advice of goods or materials to be received and their expected delivery date (Thomas H Howell Limited).

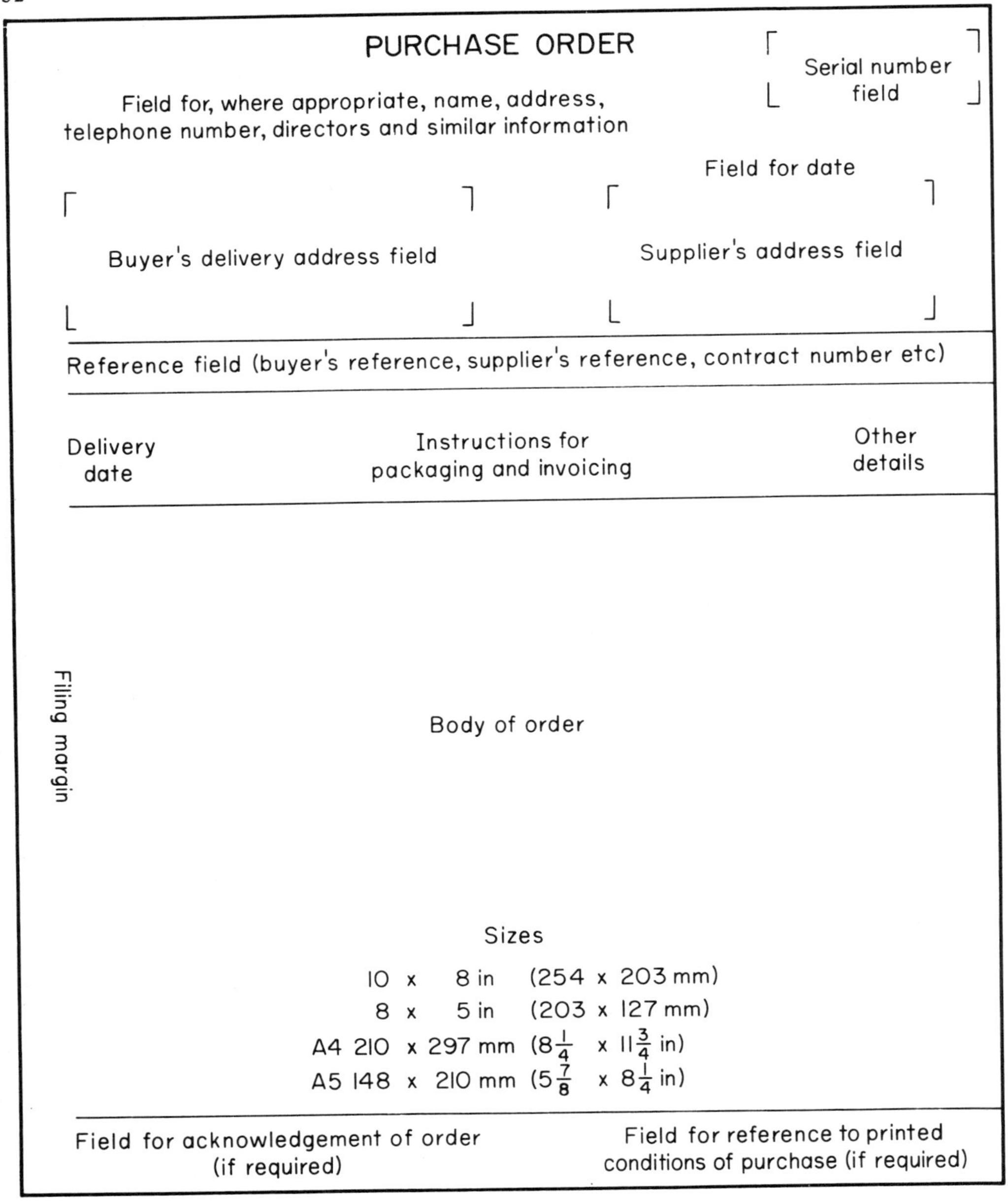

PURCHASE ORDER

⌐ Serial number
  ⌊ field ⌋

Field for, where appropriate, name, address,
telephone number, directors and similar information

Field for date

⌐   ⌐
Buyer's delivery address field   Supplier's address field

⌊   ⌊

Reference field (buyer's reference, supplier's reference, contract number etc)

| Delivery date | Instructions for packaging and invoicing | Other details |

Filing margin

Body of order

Sizes

10 x	8 in	(254 x 203 mm)
8 x	5 in	(203 x 127 mm)
A4 210 x 297 mm	$(8\frac{1}{4}$ x $11\frac{3}{4}$ in)
A5 148 x 210 mm	$(5\frac{7}{8}$ x $8\frac{1}{4}$ in)

| Field for acknowledgement of order (if required) | Field for reference to printed conditions of purchase (if required) |

Figure 4.3   Purchase order format recommended by the British Standards Institution.
The horizontal lines, which are not necessarily printed on actual forms, indicate the division of the form into a number of fields. Dimensions of the fields depend on circumstances, such as the amount of information to be entered and the method of entry.

Quantity	Description	Price

[Univac Division]

THIS PURCHASE ORDER NUMBER MUST APPEAR on all invoices, advice notes, cases, bundles, packing lists and correspondence

[Reference number]

[Sperry Rand Limited]

OFFICIAL PURCHASE ORDER

To

Date _____

Terms	Delivery instructions	Total price

Consign to	Mail invoice to Accounting Manager	For and on behalf of
Department	Requisition number	Account

Acknowledgement of receipt of order

Upon receipt of the above order please detach sign and return this acknowledgement at once to

[Univac Division Sperry Rand Limited]
[London E C I]

We hereby acknowledge receipt of order and agree to furnish
[Reference number] material specified
in exact accordance with the description of your order

Date received	Our order number
Signed	
By	Date

Figure 4.4 A neat and simple purchase order similar in style and size to the company's letterhead and all other stationery.

ORDER

Telegrams _____

Telephone _____

Order date	
Order number	
Code	Inquiry date

Department

Please supply goods as detailed
below subject to conditions set
out below and overleaf

**Goods to be delivered and
labelled to** ⟶

Stock number	Description	Quantity	Price

Repair code	Delivery date	Your quotation	Carriage	Terms of payment

Due for delivery

Date urged	Delivery promised	Date urged	Delivery promised

Item	Date	Progress by	New promise	Item	Date	Progress by	New promise

Figure 4.5 Copies of purchase order showing how the bottom space is used for progressing purposes.
This part of the form does not, of course, appear on the original purchase order sent to the supplier. It might contain, for example, authorised signatures and, perhaps, conditions of purchase.

PURCHASE REQUISITION			
		Department _____	
To purchase department: Please obtain the undermentioned		Date _____ _____ Number _____ ____	
Suggested supplier	Quantity and description	Price	Required for
	Requisitioned by	Authorised by	

Figure 4.6   A simple requisition form easy to understand by the busiest employees.
It is not advisable to have requisitions pre-printed with numbers because it might complicate checking, filing and references.

[Pfizer]
<u>Engineering stock order</u>

Supplier   Order number _____

Date _____

Code number	Material description	Quantity ordered	Unit cost	Suppliers use	Quantity received	Store use
				Quantity dispatched		

Copies: White copy (2) Supplier
          Green copy (I) Buying office
          Pink copy   (I) Stock control
          Blue copy   (I) Stores

Order approved

Stock controller _____

Buying department _____

All queries to be addressed to stock control, [Pfizer Limited]

Figure 4.7   Requisition/purchase order form.
Five copies are made, two for the supplier, one for progressing and checking completion, one for stock control analysis and one for stores (Pfizer).

PURCHASE REQUISITION CARD   Card number

Classification_____   Minimum stock_____

Code number_____ Description _____ Average monthly consumption _____

Approved suppliers   Contract   Inquiries issued

Date	Present stock	Quantity required	Unit	Delivery wanted	Required for	Approvals	Date received purchasing department	Purchase order number	Supplier	Price	Carriage	Settlement terms

Figure 4.8   Travelling requisition.
To initiate a purchase, the left hand portion is filled in and approved by an authorised person who signs in the approvals column. The right hand columns are completed when the order is placed and the terms confirmed. The columns continue on the reverse side.

Part number				Description											Drawing number		
Specifications											Supersedes						

TRAVELLING REQUISITION

| 1 | | | | | | | 3 | | | | | | | | | | |
| 2 | | | | | | | 4 | | | | | | | | | | |

Stock on hand	Requisitioned				Ordered from vendor or plant							Date promised	Received			
	Date	Quantity	Date wanted	Approved	Date	Order number	Quantity	Vendor	Cost	Per	FOB		Date	Quantity	Date	Quantity

Usage														Used on
Months	Jan	Feb	Mar	Apr	May	June	July	Aug	Sep	Oct	Nov	Dec	Total	
19														
19														
19														

Figure 4.9   Kardex travelling requisition (Remington Rand).

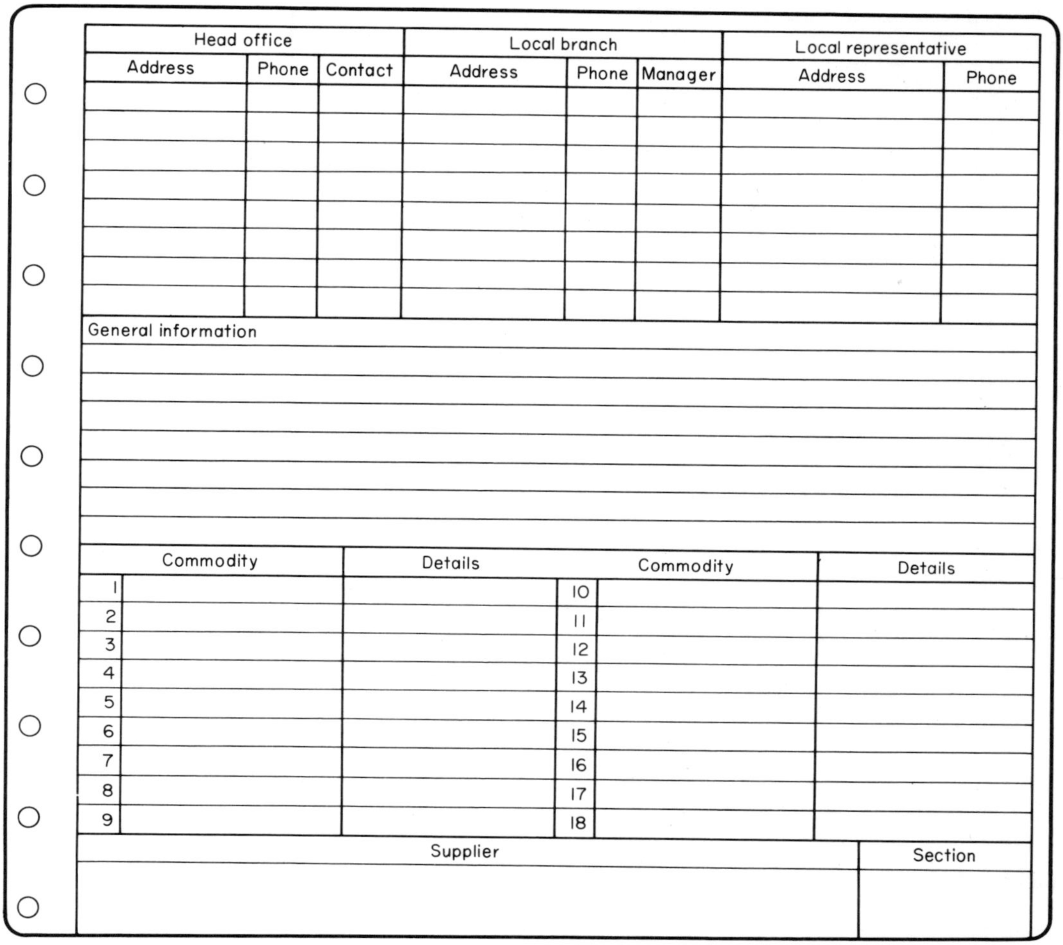

Head office			Local branch			Local representative	
Address	Phone	Contact	Address	Phone	Manager	Address	Phone

General information

Commodity	Details		Commodity	Details
1		10		
2		11		
3		12		
4		13		
5		14		
6		15		
7		16		
8		17		
9		18		

Supplier	Section

Figure 4.10   Supplier record.

Date	Order	Quantity	Supplier	Price	Delivery	Complete	Remarks

PURCHASE RECORD

Supplier_____ Material code_____

Description _____ Used for_____

Terms _____

Order number	Date	Ordered	Contract	Delivered	Balance	Delivery	Price	Invoice passed

PURCHASE RECORD

Description _____   Drawing number_____

_____   Specification_____

_____   Product_____

_____

Date	Order number	Quantity	Supplier	Price	Per	Delivery	Code	Comments

Figure 4.11   Purchase history records.
Three essentially similar buying records used by three different firms. Each form is printed on both sides of five by eight inch cards and filed in index boxes.

Supplier		Supplier	
S1		S7	
S2		S8	
S3		S9	
S4		S10	
S5		S11	
S6		S12	

Item		Relevant information	Current details				Current details			
			Date	S	Price and terms	M	Date	S	Price and terms	M
1										
2										
3										
4										
5										
6										
7										
8										
9										
10										

Description	Section	Code

M—Method of purchasing

IN	Inquiry	EST	Established price
C and NO	Contract	PH	Phone
CAT	Catalogue	PAP	Please advise price

Figure 4.12 Purchase history records designed for use in a visible-edge index binder.

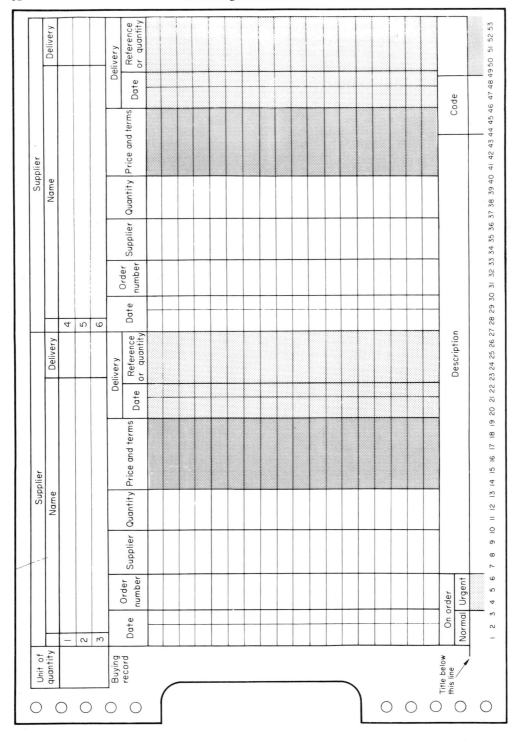

Figure 4.13   Purchase history record.
A visible-edge record form with facility for signalling progress dates along the bottom edge
(Kalamazoo).

Date _____

Dear Sirs,

Please quote, by return, your lowest price, discount and
terms for the equipment/materials specified on the attached
documents and state your earliest guaranteed delivery period
to destination from date of order.

Our general conditions are printed on the reverse side of
this letter and any special conditions relating to any
order which may result from this inquiry are contained on
the attached document.

Yours faithfully,

for _____

Figure 4.14   Standard quotation letter.

5

Stock Control Systems and Documents

Stock control is more than just taking inventory of the physical assets of the company, although this is of course necessary. Modern inventory management is concerned with reducing the total investment in stock. This can be done by careful control of purchasing quantities, as has already been suggested.

It is also necessary to reduce the variety of individual items held, which in turn reduces the number of forms and the paperwork involved in stock control.

Not infrequently an entirely new item is requisitioned and continuously stocked despite the fact that a similar item already in stock would have served the purpose. A materials index or catalogue of some sort informing employees of what is in stock should help to avoid this type of duplication.

In the same way stock lines can be reduced by limiting the different models or types of equipment purchased. By standardising the typewriter models, for example, a firm can cut down on the different sizes of ribbons it is necessary to stock. Too often it would seem that the choice of typewriter is left to the whim of the typist and a multitude of ribbon sizes must continue to be stocked long after she has left. One large firm found they were stocking some 750 grades or brands of typewriter ribbon for this very reason.

Stock control records can also be used to establish the frequeency and timing of purchase orders as well as the quantity, by analysing the usage rates of each item. This is becoming increasingly important as the time lag between the placing of orders with suppliers and delivery becomes longer and longer. Moreover, the rise in industrial disputes and increasing delays in transportation are making it that much more difficult to determine just how far in advance goods can be ordered without creating an unnecessary surplus. It is also worth considering the potential savings in using slower and less costly delivery methods which can only be done by extending the lead time—the time it takes to obtain goods from the time they are requisitioned.

The point being made is that a company can no longer leave its entire inventory control and purchasing policies to the storeman. Orders, and in particular those crucial to production or operations, must be related to works output planning and schedules or sales forecast. It is unreasonable for replenishments to be ordered only when the storeman gets around to checking existing stock and decides to inform the office. This requires well kept records and may well create more paperwork—and resentment from those involved—but the saving and improved efficiency undoubtedly make it all worthwhile.

Adequate documentation, moreover, should also help to improve security. Most firms invariably discover goods disappearing with no indication whether it is through carelessness, misdirection or through pilferage, and fraud. Good records show up deficiencies and discrepancies immediately so that they are effectively limited.

Establishing the degree of control

It is neither desirable nor practicable to maintain the same degree of control on all items. Stocks of paper clips do not need to be controlled as tightly as stocks of vehicle tyres, for example. Many firms implement a single system to their entire inventory on the basis that it is suitable to the major part of the inventory. This is an absolute waste both in terms of paperwork and the time required to complete and process the documents involved.

To improve stock turn, attention should be directed to those items representing the largest financial investment, not to the average stock. It is estimated that, on average, something like 10 to 20 per cent of the items in stock in a company account for about 80 per cent or more of the total value.

Obviously, control should be established on a graduated basis according to the usage value of each item.

Stores checks should be much more frequent and tolerances much tighter on the more expensive items, for example. In the same way, deliveries of the more costly items can be made less frequently, possible on a call-off basis under contract, to minimise inventory and holding costs, not to mention pilferage.

Preparation of materials index

To begin with a company should, of course, know what is in stock and the value for accounting purposes. It is helpful if the inventory lists complement another index, in purchasing or accounts for example. If possible there should be a single code number for each item and the same system of identification used on all documents. The code used in a materials index, for example, should be linked with the bought ledger coding.

In some firms, though it is preferable to use manufacturers' parts numbers. Others devise their own coding system, identifying items according to categories which are further sub-divided according to different characteristics in descending order of importance. One company, for example, codes each item with an eight-digit number, the first two digits indicating the class and group, and the last four breaking down the category more specifically by size, length, material, radius, shape and so on. Code numbers are assigned with gaps of five or ten for every item to allow new items to be inserted in their logical place.

This helps to identify unnecessary duplication of stock items and provides a basic index which can be used to include more comprehensive data on each item.

Once a materials index is completed it can be duplicated to obviate the need to write out each item when taking inventory. In firms with a limited range of goods it may be practicable to print a basic list of the type of goods or categories on sale slips, purchase orders and so on, so that only the quantity needs to be entered (see Figure 6.3).

Stock balance record

Individual record cards can be used to record the quantity held on each item, issues and receipts, and the resulting balance. This provides the actual stock position on any item at any time, and eases the burden of annual stocktaking with all the trouble and major dislocation which this usually entails. Moreover it is possible to obtain from the issues the pattern of usage of each item over a period of time. At the same time it calls to attention much sooner than could otherwise be hoped losses due to wastage or pilferage and enables action to be taken promptly. In the event of fire, a current inventory record of stock is of immense value and enables an insurance claim to be met more quickly.

A stock balance record normally contains the name of item, the part number or other identification, location of the item or bin number and columns for *In*, *Out* and *Balance* and possibly for dates and reference numbers. Figures 5.1 and 5.2 are examples of this type of record.

Many firms issue forms such as the one shown in Figure 5.3 which are used to withdraw items from stores, and the total issue of each item is prepared from these and recorded only once instead of each time an item is drawn. This method is particularly useful where items drawn from stores are numerous.

In calculating stock balance it is important to remember any stock which has already been allocated but not issued. This can be done by simply adding another column on the stock balance card for recording allocations. Figure 5.4 is an example of such a form.

The ledger forms illustrated in Figures 5.5 and 5.6 have columns for recording the value of items issued and received as well as the stock balance.

Order Levels

Each stock balance record normally contains the re-order level and the item is automatically requistioned whenever the balance approaches this level. In some instances it is easier or more meaningful if the order level is expressed in terms of time rather than quantity. For example, if the current rate of usage is fifty a day, and the buffer stock is to be one hundred items, this would be expressed as two days' stock.

Very often minimum and maximum quantity levels are also recorded on the stock balance card. The first indicates the minimum level to which the stock should be allowed to fall, so that an order may have to be urged or another urgently placed for immediate delivery.

By fixing a maximum quantity to be held on an item, the order quantity can be easily determined and the inventory is kept down. Otherwise there is a tendency for the storeman to play it safe by ordering more than enough. While he may be held at fault for shortages no one will complain of surplus stock, he may feel. In many firms, the office in turn unknowingly adds to the amount requisitioned 'just in case'.

Imprest systems   For items which do not require close attention or comprehensive records, there are other methods for triggering off re-orders. Some of these methods may be considered crude but the important thing is that they work. They usually involve the transfer of goods from reserve to forward stock.

One way is to place the buffer stock in a sealed container of some sort with a requisition slip. When working stock has been used up, the storekeeper breaks open the container and sends the requisition slip, containing the item number and the quantity to be ordered, to the office. A variation of this system is one in which two bins are used, the second to be used only when the first is emptied and a requisition order is placed.

Another method is to rule the inside of a bin to indicate the minimum order level, and a new order is placed when stock in the bin falls low enough for the ruled line to be visible. Often the inside of the bin is painted a bright colour below the line for emphasis.

Setting order levels   The size of the buffer stock is determined by two principal factors: the usage rate and the lead time, that is the total time it takes to obtain an item from the time a purchase requisition is first made. A safety stock may also be included to safeguard against fluctuations in demand, industrial disputes at suppliers, transportation difficulties, and so on. The economic order quantity (see page 41) is another factor to be taken into consideration.

The figure for both the lead time and usage rates change constantly and it is important that they be looked at regularly and adjusted when necessary. It may be worthwhile to make regular summaries, weekly or monthly, of crucial items at least, showing the opening balance, receipts and issues, closing balance and net movement in respect of each item.

Only quantities need be shown and any significant change in the usage rate indicated. If a particular line has increased in sales, for example, the increase should be promptly reflected so that the normal order can be increased or brought forward.

Combined stock and purchasing records

In many firms stock control and purchasing records are kept together to help ensure that all entries are made on both records. Thus, figures on each are consistent and duplication of data is avoided. In some firms details regarding purchases and stock are integrated on a single card. Figure 5.7 shows an example of a very basic purchasing/stock control record.

Examples of purchasing and stock control forms designed to complement each other and kept together are illustrated in Figures 5.8 and 5.9. Both are intended as visible edge records.

The first is fairly self-explanatory. The facing card is a basic purchasing record card, but with a section on the far right to record the total of stock issues for each month. This enables the clerk to evaluate increases/decreases of an item over previous years to ensure that the stock for the current year is at a realistic level. The main insert card contains the basic *In, Out* and *Balance* columns. At the end of every month the *Out* column is totalled and the figure is inserted in the appropriate section on the facing card. The visible edge title insert contains minimum and maximum stock levels, part number, description and bin location.

The second record card, Figure 5.9, has all the basic ingredients of the previous record but with additional features. For example, the facing card is split into two—*Purchasing* and *Monthly usage and suppliers* The reason for two cards is that because more entries are made on the first it is completed sooner than the other. The split facing cards make it more economical to order.

On the stock card is inserted an extra column *Total month to date* which is a cumulative presentation of stock issued for one month. This saves time in adding at the end of each month. The final figures need only to be inserted on the appropriate facing card.

The most significant difference between the two records is that the second shows the actual physical stock situation on the visible edge. This is done by a graphic computing chart together with a telescopic signal. The range is from 1 to 200 and even if items of stock are in the thousands, this can be shown by using a different coloured telescopic signal. In other words a different coloured signal would be taken to indicate 9000 to 12000 units instead of 900 to 1200.

Usage records

While stock balance records provide a record of items issued, other sources are needed to obtain a record of actual usage and to provide a good cross-check of stock balance records.

A daily analysis of sales by unit, model number, size, colour and so on can be recorded from sales slips and invoices. Figure 5.10 shows an example of an invoice designed for keeping stock control records. In manufacturing concerns, job cards and works orders can be used in the same way. If each product uses the same number of components, only the production reports are needed.

Assessing the annual usage value

By multiplying the annual usage of each item by the item cost to obtain the annual usage value it is possible to classify each item and establish the necessary controls. This can be done simply as shown in Figure 5.11. All items should then be listed according to annual usage value, beginning with the largest on top and the smallest at the bottom. Two extra columns can be included on the form illustrated, one to show the percentage of total number of items covered up to each line, and the percentage which these items contribute to the total annual usage value. If a separate card is used for each item it is easier to place them in order. Alternatively, the items can be arranged in groups and summarised in the same way, that is, according to the annual usage value, on a shorter list.

The total inventory is then divided with about ten per cent of the items in class *A* to which the greatest attention should be given, about five per cent in class *B* and the remainder in class *C*. Another method is to take the average usage value and multiply it by six to get the boundary between class *A* and *B*. The boundary between class *B* and class *C* is taken as half the average usage value. This is a very quick and rather rough method and the classifications may have to be adjusted in the light of experience or when a sample analysis or a complete analysis is made later, but it would give a starting point.

Different coloured record cards can be used to indicate the category an item belongs to. For example:

> Green for items valued at less than £5
> Blue for items valued at between £5 and £50
> Pink for items valued at between £50 and £500
> Red for items valued at over £500

Minimum stock levels and re-order quantities can then be set only for each of the four grades, based on average use and the lead time for each component.

The data necessary for grouping items can normally be obtained from past stock and purchasing records or other resources. Usage rates and prices should be kept under constant surveillance, however, and items regrouped if the annual usage value changes.

Recording and control of goods received

A proper stock control system, to be effective, must cover the whole of the material flow, including receipt and despatch of goods.

Basically it is necessary to know when goods are received, the quantity and whether or not they are in good condition. Stock control records should be updated as soon as the goods are received.

Despatch documents.   Most firms require that a packing statement or advice note be sent with the goods giving details of batch numbers or net weights. As has already been indicated, this enables the customer to check the contents of the parcel on delivery. A set of delivery or consignment notes is also usually made out to accompany the goods delivered to a customer. There are normally two copies of this document, one of which is signed by the customer on accepting delivery and returned to the office.

Claims of non-delivery of goods to a customer are commonplace and without this third copy, signed by the recipient, there is no basis on which to contest the claim. The signed copy of the delivery document should be filed and retaind for a period sufficient to preclude loss possibilities of any claims made. Six months is a reasonable time. There may be no dishonesty on the part of the customer, whose own records may be faulty, but he will be convinced he is right in the absence of proof to the contrary.

Goods received documents.   A record of goods received is usually noted on a copy of the purchase order which is provided to the receiving bay for this purpose. Alternatively, the goods can be recorded on a summary sheet and the supplier's advice note or goods received note approved and sent to the office. Figure 5.12 shows an example of a goods received note.

Before approving goods received, however, the advice note or goods delivery note should be checked against the original purchase order to ensure that the goods have in fact been ordered and are in accordance with the order. In many firms a copy of each purchase order is sent to the receiving bay for this purpose. Approval can be noted on this order copy, which can be easily married up with the copy in the progress file or accounts.

If no purchase order can be found, a check should be made whether or not the goods come from a regular supplier and, if so, whether he can quote his authorisation. If the goods are normally used by one person in particular, however, it may be worth checking with him first.

In some firms, payment for goods is authorised by the person who originally requisitioned the goods after he has inspected them. In these circumstances the originator of the requisition should receive a copy of the purchase order or retain a copy of the requisition on which to note his authorisation for payment.

As it is important that everyone concerned is notified of goods delivered, a special set of forms is often completed for this purpose on receipt of goods. This also obviates the need to find the original order at point of delivery, which may hold up the flow of incoming goods (see Figure 5.12).

The order number can be obtained from a summary of orders provided by the office, listing each order placed each day in order number.

Smart and Brown Lighting Limited uses a five part set of goods received forms (see Figure 5.13) which are divided and processed as follows:

Part 1 is normally routed to the buyer for checking against the purchase order and, pending receipt of a good report from the inspection department, authority for payment against invoice.

Parts 2 and 3 are passed with the goods to Inspection. The goods are examined and, when passed, the inspection copy is signed and forwarded to the buyer. The stores copy meanwhile passes with the goods to stores and is used for updating stock records.

The goods received note (part 4) is held in the Goods Inwards department as a record of all items which have been checked in through their receiving bays.

The accounts copy (part 5) is sent straight to the accounts department. Pending receipt of notification from the buyer, this copy is an authority for payment.

Some firms design their purchase orders to serve as goods received notes. This is an excellent system where orders are completed with a single delivery but is unsuitable when a large number of deliveries may be made against the order. An example of a combined purchase order/goods received note is shown in Figure 5.14.

Godfrey Philips, cigarette tobacco manufacturers, use a single document which not only combines the purchase order and the goods received note, but serves as a purchase record card, as a supplier quotation record and as a supplier quality record as well (see Figure 5.15).

The basic document is a dyeline system translucent master size fifteen by ten inches, which is filed under an item code cross referenced to a material description chart. With this system, the practice of giving a new code for each supplier or a minor specification change was discontinued. The following information is typed on the master:

1   Name and address of supplier
2   Material code
3   Item description/specification
4   Where the material is or how the material is used.

This translucent master is filed in the item files until the item requires re-ordering, much like a travelling requisition. At this time, a submaster of the same size is made out on a dyeline copier and the original master is immediately refiled in the item file until the time to order. The submaster then has the following information entered on it:

1   Addition of a prefix or suffix
2   Order number and order date. This appears twice, once on the body of the form and once on the acknowledgement slip, so that when it is returned it is clear which order it refers to
3   Quantity required
4   Delivery information
5   Price details
6   Any special instructions—confirmation order, proofs required and
7   Authority for order
8   Names and addresses of suppliers asked to quote.

On completion of this data, two copies are produced from the submaster, one of the purchase order section, which is sent to the supplier, and a copy of the whole document for office use. The submaster goes to the receiving department and stock controllers who, after annotating their own records, keep the submasters in date order.

When the goods are received or partly received, the date, quantity received and the balance of the order are recorded on the GRN part of the submaster. This document then serves as the GRN. There is no need to write out the stores code, the name of the supplier or the material description. If the order is complete, this copy is approved for payment and filed. If the order is incomplete, two copies are made of the entire document, one for accounts for payment, the second to replace the original document in the item file and the submaster is returned to stores.

Stock records for security purposes

Great care must be taken to ensure that goods do not disappear, particularly between manufacturing and dispatch.

Various checks can be made on the flow of goods between the two departments but these checks are not usually successful, partly due to goods left unsecured at night or during breaks.

Any loss will be reflected in the departmental budget by simply comparing the total of goods sold with the quantity recorded on the packing statements. In companies where there is an inspection or quality control staff measuring the quantity and quality of goods as they flow from manufacturing their records will prove to be another good source of control information (and, incidentally, show the extent to which production capacity is being utilised).

J. Lyons use a simple production control system consisting of a control sheet and a set of overlapped pallet loading slips in duplicate, each of which has carbon strip on the reverse side. When a pallet becomes full, the operator completes the top pallet loading slip, detailing the code number of the product, number of the pallet, operator's name, and date and number of the slip series. These details reproduce on to the duplicate copy of the slip and on the back of both slips. The control sheet is finally headed up with the machine number.

As each pallet passes from the packing department a checker takes stock of the number of orders on each pallet and confirms this with the pallet loading slip. If there is an obvious discrepancy, the pallet is withdrawn for investigation; otherwise the details on the slip are transferred to a packing check sheet. As each pallet arrives in the dispatch department the same procedure is carried out, and at intervals during the day the respective clerks compare their check sheets. If the two sheets agree each sheet is signed by the other clerk.

The opportunity for fraud most frequently arises at the consignment note stage. Instances have occured where goods in excess of an order have been deliberately labelled and consigned to a dishonest customer. This has even been known where no legitimate order of any kind has been in existence.

This is a good reason why all documents concerned with despatch should be interlinked with the original order. If despatch documents can be created in a warehouse without the other notes coming into existence, it might be possible to conceal the methods of goods getting out, because the automatic procedural action, which would normally follow outside that department, would never begin. The existence of an interlinked system where warehouse staff could only dispatch in accordance with notes sent to them would eliminate this possibility.

Transport schedule for goods delivery

A vehicle and driver scheduling sheet may need to be prepared for arranging delivery of goods (see Figure 5.16). To do this it may be necessary to list the goods which need to be delivered, quantified by weight or capacity unit, the unit/load requirement for each day, the daily unit totals, and the unit totals over a period. From this it is possible to isolate the types of goods or articles to be carried each day.

One must know the physical restrictions of vehicle weight, lengths, heights and widths, of course, and it may be helpful to keep a record of these in the office. It is also important that the person arranging deliveries is informed of vehicles which for one reason or another are inoperative.

Scheduled deliveries can be noted against each order on a daily order summary used to indicate when transport is available for despatch, and the customer should receive an acknowledgement accordingly.

In larger firms, it may be useful to keep a control board which indicates the movement of every vehicle, its location, whether it is loaded or awaiting loading, whether it is in transit or whether it has arrived at its destination, and if it has when it will be unloaded. A different card can be used for each vehicle and inserted in the appropriate columns.

Special insurance conditions

Where high risk goods are carried in company vehicles special conditions and limitations are certain to be applied by any standard insurance cover and the company must ensure that these are complied with as claims may be invalidated. For example, an insurance policy may exclude loss or damage by theft while the van is left unattended in a public place, unless securely locked.

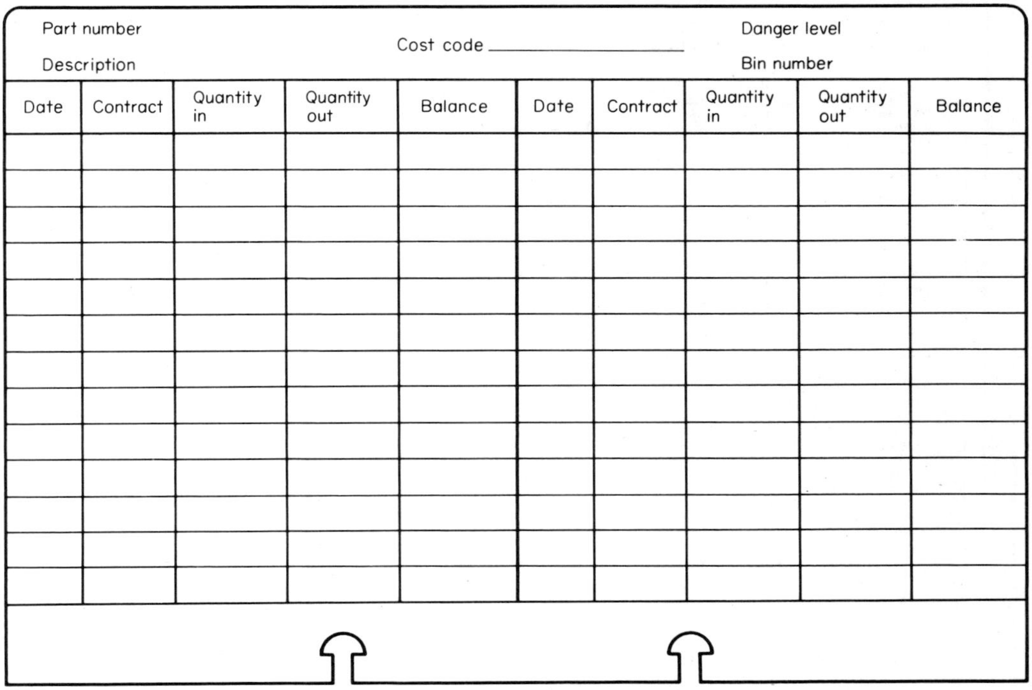

Part number				Cost code _____				Danger level		
Description								Bin number		
Date	Contract	Quantity in	Quantity out	Balance	Date	Contract	Quantity in	Quantity out	Balance

Figure 5.1 Stock and record card.
A standard record card designed for a rotary index file (C W Cave).

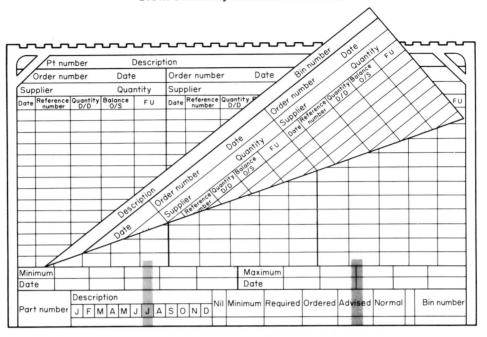

Figure 5.2   Stock control record card.
A Kardex visible-index card (Remington Rand).

STORES ISSUE/REQUISITION						

		Job number			Date		
		Department or requisition number			Returnable	Yes	No
	£ value	Quantity	Stock number	Description			Bin number
		Issued by		Received by		Stock records up dated	

Figure 5.3   Stores issue requisition form.
This document can be used either as a stores issue or requisition. As a stock issue, the document is completed with the requirements, authorised and signed by the workman as a receipt for goods issued. The original is filed in the department which requisitioned the items and a duplicate is filed in stores, where details are entered in a stock ledger. As a stores requisition, the original of the document is kept in the stores and the duplicate by the originating department (Lamson Paragon).

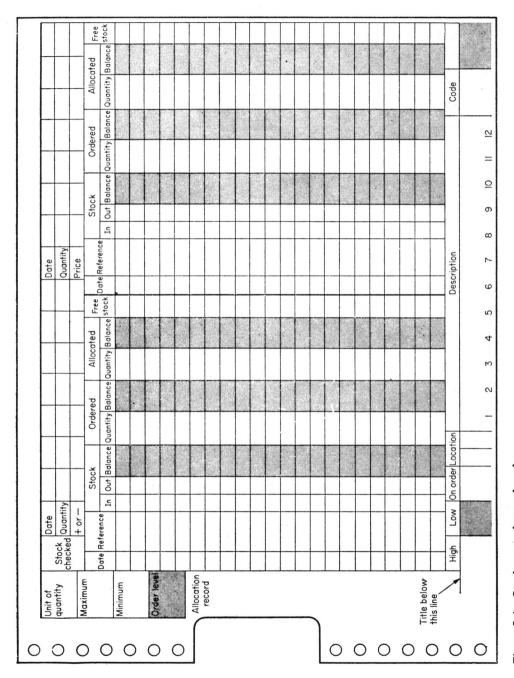

Figure 5.4 Stock control record card.

A visible-index form with additional columns for recording allocations. Note also the space at the top of the form for recording physical stocktaking and discrepancies (Kalamazoo).

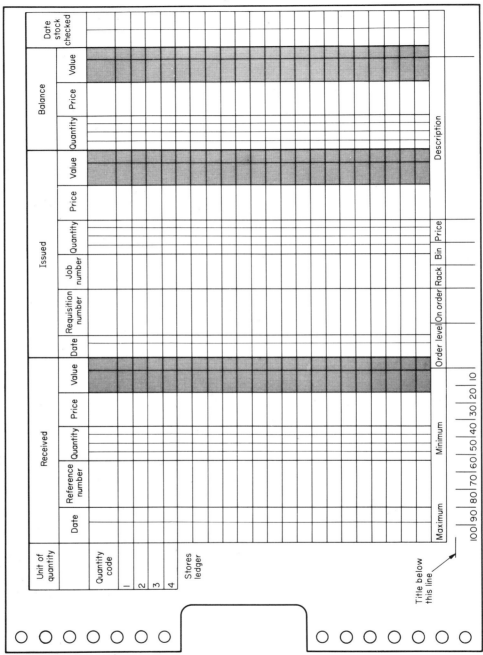

Figure 5.5 Stock control ledger form.
A standard visible-ledger form. (Kalamazoo).

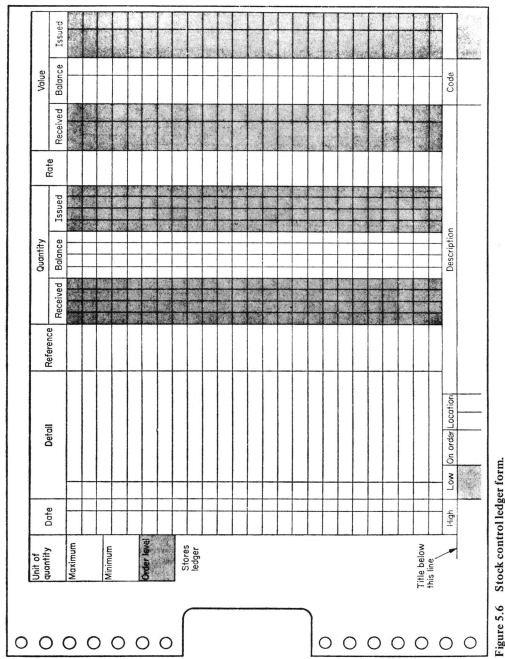

Figure 5.6 Stock control ledger form.
A visible-index form with an additional column on the right for recording goods received and issued, and the balance in terms of value (Kalamazoo.)

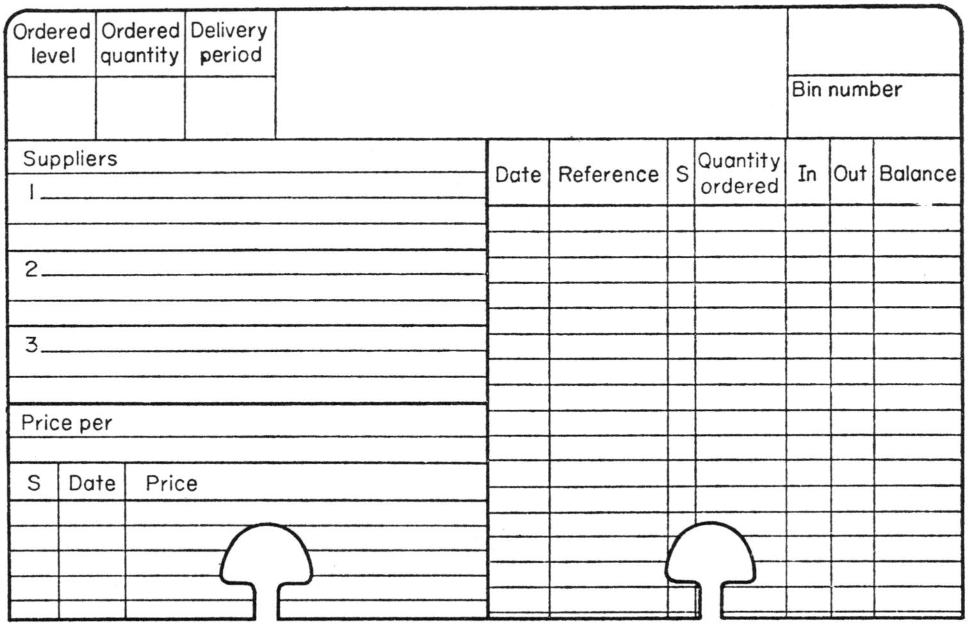

Ordered level	Ordered quantity	Delivery period							Bin number		
				Date	Reference	S	Quantity ordered	In	Out	Balance	
Suppliers											
1											
2											
3											
Price per											
S	Date	Price									

Figure 5.7   Stock control/purchasing record (C W Cave).

Part number		Description											
Number		Suppliers			Number				Number		Suppliers		
I					3				5				
2					4				6				
Delivery to commence			at rate of			PURCHASES							
Date	Supp	Order number	Quantity	Price	Date	Quantity received	Balance order/sheet	Inventory value	Remarks	Month	19	19	19
									Jan				
									Feb				
									Mar				
									Apr				
									May				
									June				
									July				
									Aug				
									Sept				
									Oct				
									Nov				
									Dec				
									Total				

Part number			Description					Bin number			Card number			
Date	Reference	In	Out	Balance	Date	Reference	In	Out	Balance	Date	Reference	In	Out	Balance
Minimum					Minimum									
Date					Date									

Part number	Description												Nil	Minimum	Required	Ordered	Advised	Normal	Bin number
	Jan	Feb	Mar	Apl	May	Jun	July	Aug	Sep	Oct	Nov	Dec							

Figure 5.8   Kardex purchase record (top) and stock control (bottom) cards.
Each card is printed in the same way on both sides. The 'supp' column under 'PURCHASES' on the facing card refers to the supplier, who is identified by the appropriate code number. On the visible edge are transparent control signals. A green signal moves from the 'Normal' section to the 'Minimum' when minimum level is reached. At the end of the day the operator runs down the visible edge to assess those items to be requisitioned. The signal moves to 'Required' and the item is ordered. Details are recorded on the purchase card, the signal is moved to 'Ordered' and a red signal inserted in the 'Jan' to 'Dec' scale to signify month of ordering. During this period, stock is still being issued and if it reaches a critical level the supplier has to be chased—the green signal moving to 'Advised'. When stock is received entries are made on the 'PURCHASES' section and the stock card. The green signal moves to 'Normal' and the red signal is removed (Remington Rand).

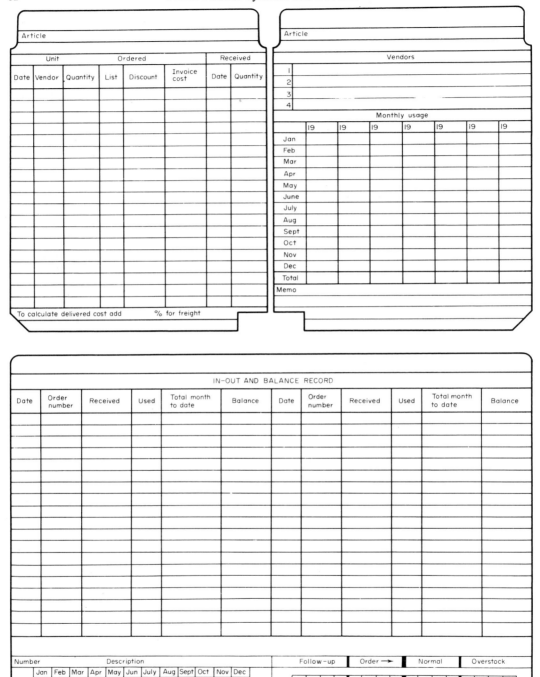

Figure 5.9   Stock control/purchasing record for a rotary index file (C W Cave).

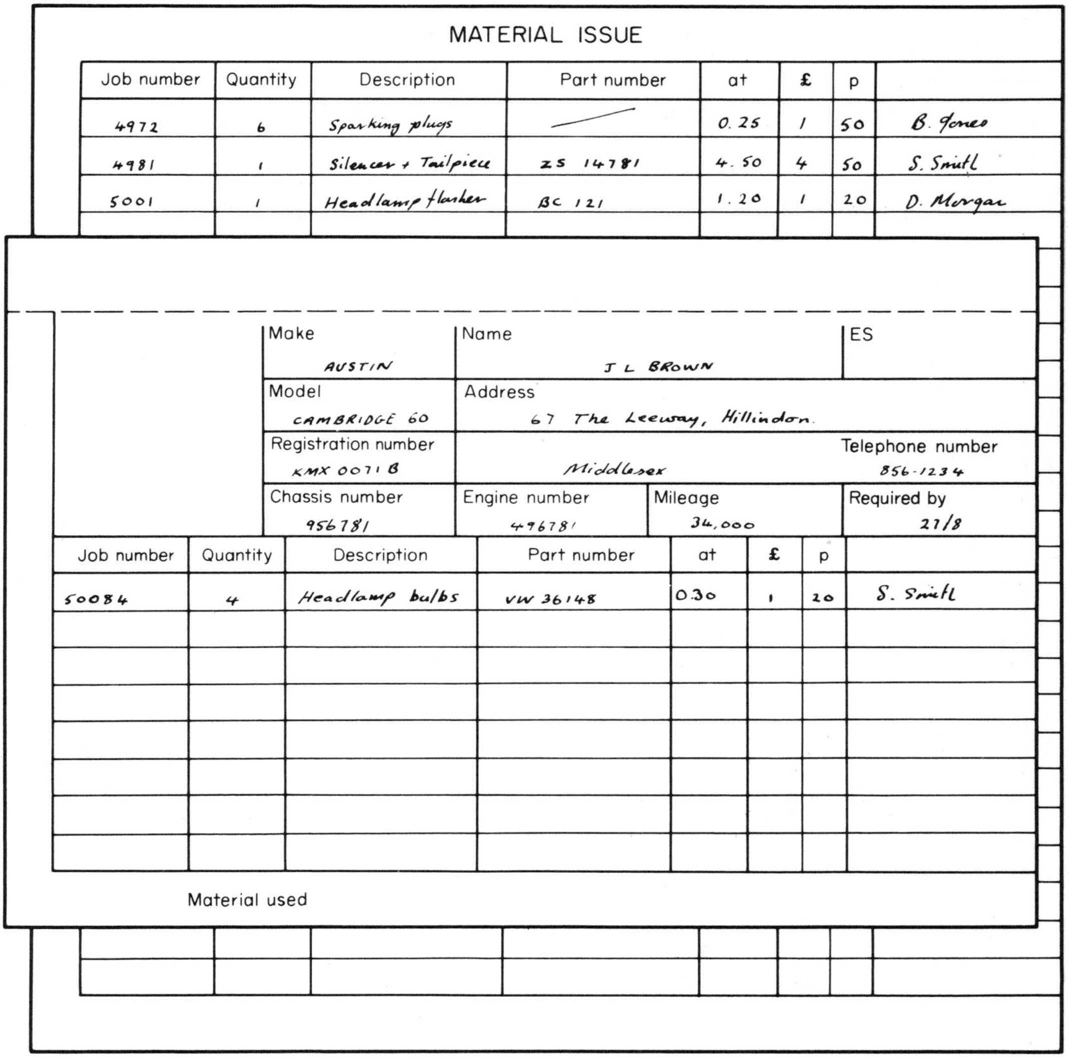

MATERIAL ISSUE

Job number	Quantity	Description	Part number	at	£	p	
4972	6	Sparking plugs		0.25	1	50	B. Jones
4981	1	Silencer + Tailpiece	ZS 14781	4.50	4	50	S. Smith
5001	1	Headlamp Flasher	BC 121	1.20	1	20	D. Morgan

Make	Name		ES
AUSTIN	J L BROWN		

Model	Address
CAMBRIDGE 60	67 The Leeway, Hillindon.

Registration number		Telephone number
KMX 0071 B	Middlesex	856-1234

Chassis number	Engine number	Mileage	Required by
956781	476781	34,000	27/8

Job number	Quantity	Description	Part number	at	£	p	
50084	4	Headlamp bulbs	VW 36148	0.30	1	20	S. Smith

Material used

Figure 5.10   Invoice/material issue form system.
These forms were designed for use with the Lamson three-in-one register so that each entry on the invoice is recorded simultaneously on the stores copy. The carbon paper covering the stores issue form has been removed for the purpose of the illustration (Lamson Paragon).

Part number	Usage quantity	Unit cost	Usage value
P1234	500	1	500
P1235	5	100	500
P1236	10,000	.05	500
P1237	1,000	.05	50

Figure 5.11   Annual usage value summary.

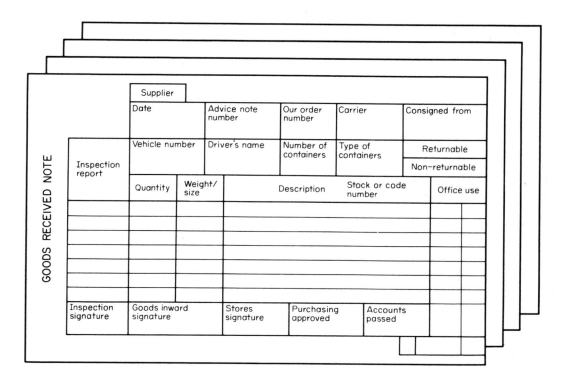

Figure 5.12   Goods received note.
A standard stock form available from Lamson Paragon for use on their counter registers (Lamson Paragon).

GOODS RECEIVED NOTE					
Supplier	Advice note number	Purchase order number	Case number	Discrepancy note number	
Address	Carrier	Date goods received	Chargeable packing	Date	

Description of goods	Part number	Advised	Received	Accepted	Rejected	Stock

PURCHASING DEPARTMENT

Receiving dock signature	Inspection signature	Release note number	Stores count	Date	Entered on stock control	Date
Date	Date	Batch number	Stores signature		Debit note number	Date

Figure 5.13   Goods inward forms.
A set of forms designed by Lamson Paragon. Each copy is printed on a different coloured sheet for easy identification (Smart and Brown Lighting).

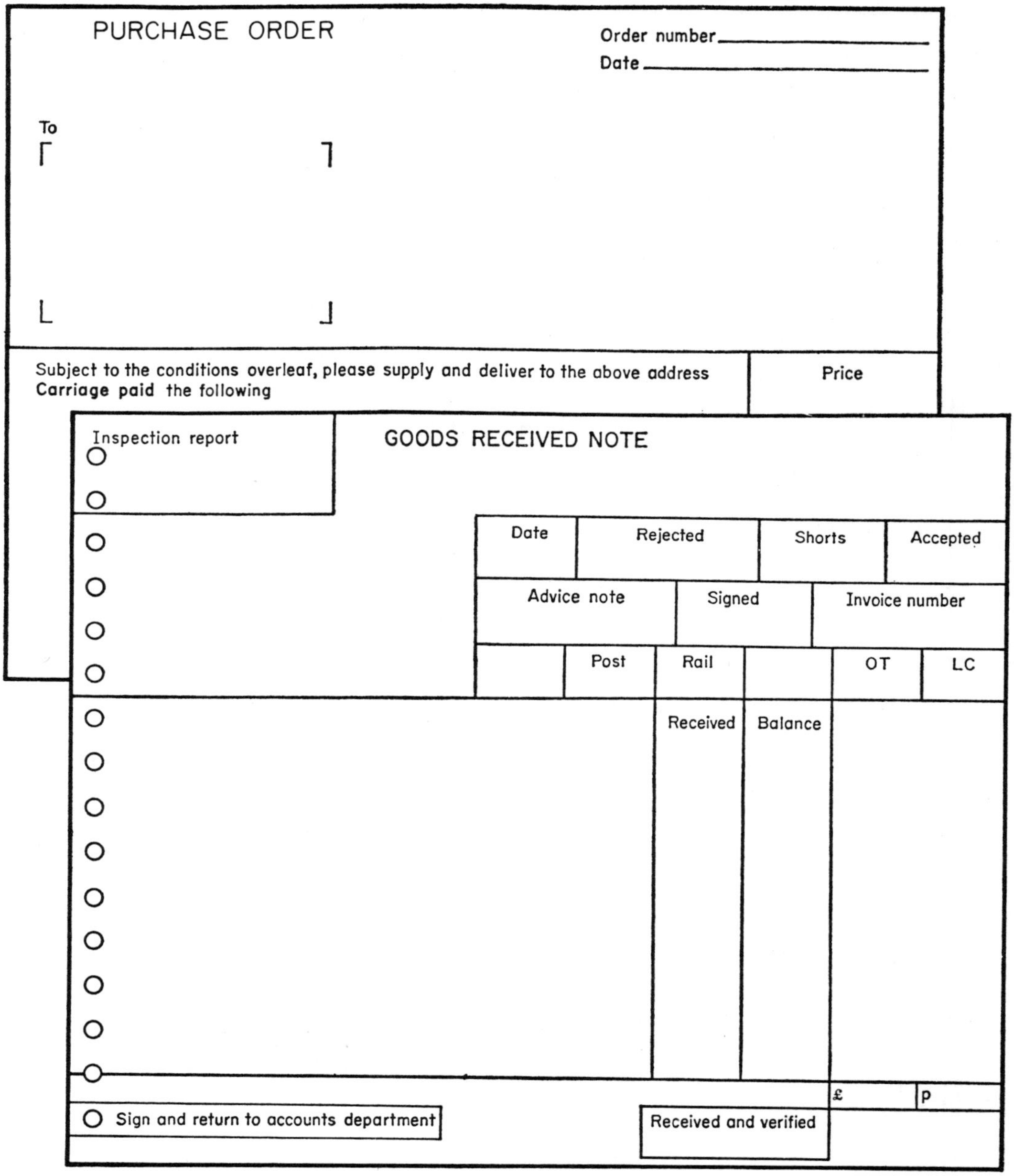

PURCHASE ORDER

Order number_____

Date_____

To

Subject to the conditions overleaf, please supply and deliver to the above address
Carriage paid the following

Price

Inspection report

GOODS RECEIVED NOTE

Date	Rejected	Shorts	Accepted
Advice note	Signed		Invoice number

	Post	Rail		OT	LC
	Received	Balance			

£ | p

Sign and return to accounts department

Received and verified

Figure 5.14 Combined purchase order and goods received note based on a form used by Mullard Research Laboratories.

[Godfrey Phillips Limited]
[London, E1]

Purchase order number

Authority for order

Where/how material used

Free stock	Stock at date	Reorder level	Average monthly usage last 6 months	Peak monthly usage last 6 months	Forecast usage rate	Price revision agreed by buyer who placed this order

Date _____
All documents relating to this order must bear the above number

To _____

Please acknowledge receipt of this order using attached slip

London factory

Goods accepted 8 am – 4 pm
Monday–Thursday, 8 am – 3.30 pm
Friday, closed each day 1–2 pm

Goods delivered and returned

Delivery forecast/progress report

Date	Quantity delivered	Quantity returned	Order Balance	First progress date

Please supply and deliver to our unloading bay unless otherwise specified

Suppliers asked to quote for this order were

Comments on quality supplied

1
2
3
4
5
6
7
8

Deliver by _____ do not deliver before _____
Do advise if unable to deliver as specified above   for _____

_____ (Purchasing officer)

We acknowledge receipt of your purchase order _____

Supply Department,
[Godfrey Phillips Limited,]
[London, E1]

We shall inform you as soon as possible if your specified delivery date cannot be met

Dated _____   Signed _____ Date _____
        for _____

Figure 5.15   Combined purchase order and purchase record form used by Godfrey Phillips.

Week commencing Monday _____						
Monday						
Tuesday						
Wednesday						
Thursday						
Friday						
Saturday						

Figure 5.16   Vehicle and drive route sheet.
A simple delivery schedule which can save time and frustration. Receipts of goods delivery notes could be checked against this schedule (Williams Spray and Son).

6

Preparation of Sales Documents

Cash sales are comparatively straightforward. Details of every transaction, including returns and credits, should be recorded, with a receipt for the customer and a copy for the company use. This is normally done automatically on a cash register or in writing on a sales slip. If goods are purchased on credit the customer's signature is obtained on the sales slip. Figures 6.1 shows examples of simple sales slips.

Goods purchased on credit or ordered involve much more paperwork, however, and good controls are required to ensure that credit is not extended to bad payers or to people unknown to the firm and that payments are made as agreed. The system necessary varies considerably from company to company depending on the nature of the business or product and the *modus operandi* of the company generally. There are, however, two documents fundamental to any good system: the order and the invoice.

Handling and recording orders

Most firms have their own sales order forms for use by their salesmen to make sure that all the necessary details are obtained, such as:

1 Name and address of customer
2 Date of the order
3 Exact description of goods
4 Quantity of goods
5 Any special conditions
6 Address where goods should be delivered if different from the one already stated
7 Space for calculating and extending the unit and total price

Copies of orders can either be circulated to the appropriate section—the works, despatch and accounts, for example—or additional copies made by each for their own use.

Orders received directly from customers must be checked to make sure that they contain all the necessary information and to note any special conditions or instructions, regarding delivery for instance, set by the customer. The order can be stamped to indicate its circulation, with boxes to be ticked as each task is completed, until it is returned to accounts for invoicing.

In some firms, orders, whether received directly from customers or from the field representatives, are numbered consecutively upon receipt and this becomes the order and invoice number.

Scholl Manufacturing Company has a commodity index consisting of nine pre-printed lists, one for each line, showing all 825 items in size order. The nine lines are overlapped on an order board so that the title part of each section is exposed, and the extreme right hand column of the fist index list is seen to be adjacent to the appropriate column on the order form below. The required quantity of each commodity is then entered in the column on the order form. The first index list is then turned back exposing the next, and the same procedure is carried out for all nine lists. The nine lists of the commodity index are then removed, leaving the order form beneath with the quantities needed showing against the appropriate item code numbers (see Figure 6.3).

Preparation and despatch of invoices

Basically an invoice contains the same information as the sales order, with perhaps the addition of any special discounts of tax, and sales terms, such as the credit period allowed. If no discount is allowed the words *Terms Net* are included. *Prompt settlement* is used when no credit period is allowed. A few firms still write E and OE meaning *errors and omissions excepted* at the foot of the invoice, but this is really unnecessary because the courts long ago decided that genuine errors in making out invoices can be corrected later.

There is a current tendency not to send out separate invoices for each order placed. Any outstanding amount is recorded on the top of each invoice, and the new amount added. Invoices are then filed in a loose-leaf binder and the top copy is mailed at the month's end. Copies of each invoice are mailed only on request. Until they are paid the outstanding copies are kept in customer sequence where they can be reviewed easily and quickly. Figure 6.4 is an example of a typical invoice.

Using sales documents for sales analyses

Regular examination of sales slips, orders and invoices provides valuable information for sales analyses for stock control purposes. It also provides a good indication of trends in sales, which is valuable for sales forecasting and establishing stock order levels, and gives a good picture of the firm's market generally.

In many firms orders are listed as received and summarised daily to calculate how much stock of each line has been sold.

Figure 5.10 shows an invoice designed so that every entry is recorded simultaneously on a materials issue list.

It is also worth scrutinising different types of orders periodically to calculate the degree of profit on each type of sale. This can be done quickly by broadly analysing the standard return on each type of order, including delivered and charged transactions, together with the standard profit in money terms and as a percentage of sales. Sales of job orders which have a profit rate below normal can then be scrutinised and those in the red investigated more thoroughly.

Order form as invoice and despatch note

Copies of an order form are occasionally used to serve as the invoice. Except that entries must be clearly legible and, if possible, printed or typed, no more work is created for the salesman than he would not ordinarily have had.

Normally the invoice is completed with the order except for the quantity actually delivered and the price extensions. These are written in after the goods have been delivered.

Thomas Wilcock and Son of Colwyn Bay, who provide spare parts to retail motor dealers, uses such a system in which dealers, in making out their purchase orders, prepare their own invoices.

Four parts are completed in fact. The dealer retains one copy for his own use, and the remaining three parts are sent to Thomas Wilcock to serve as the invoice, the packing note and the control copy. Should only a part order be supplied, this is indicated on the invoice and the other parts by the supplier, and the customer is made aware of this on receiving the packing note.

Instructions on the completion and usage of the forms are highlighted in two ways for the dealer. They are printed in reverse type and are positioned at the foot of the form, immediately beneath the dealer's signature line (see Figure 6.8).

There have been no objections from dealers because there is no additionaal work to do, and, in fact, customer loyalty has increased as a result of the new system, according to Thomas Wilcock.

In the same way additional copies of an order can be made in one writing to serve as despatch notes as well as an invoice. As the invoice must be prepared later anyway there is no reason why this cannot be done when the order is received. This not only saves time and work but obviates the possibility of an order not being invoiced. Invoices are held and sent to the customer only on receipt of the goods received note with the customer's signature.

Many firms already re-type clean all incoming orders whether from customers directly or from sales representatives, so that it is quite a simple matter to design an additional copy to serve as an invoice. There are good reasons for re-typing all incoming orders:

1   Employees concerned with fulfilling and processing order forms deal with only one form which serves as their authority and avoids misunderstandings
2   Data is always in the same format and the information is complete, or should be completed by the typist before passing on any work forms.

The number of copies varies; copies could be used for any of the following purposes:

1   Acknowledgement of order
2   Invoice
3   Day book copy
4   Delivery note
5   Receipt note
6   Works copy
7   Warehouse copy (for release of goods)
8   Packing note
9   Advice copy
10   Transport (for scheduling)
11   Sales (for analysis)
12   Sales representative

A single copy can probably serve the purpose of two or more of the above, as will be seen in the following examples.

The three-part invoice shown in Figure 6.5, for example, is completed with two copies, one used as the agent's copy and the other as a packing note with its top half perforated and with a gummed backing to serve as a parcel label.

Four part sets of sales documents

Figure 6.6 shows an example of a four-part set of invoice/delivery documents, the first part of which is used as an advice and goods note, advising the customer that a priced invoice which is to follow is in fact a copy of this advice note. In this way when the customer receives the invoice he merely has to check the prices and calculations. It is obvious that the carbon copy is the same as the advice note received with the goods.

W Spray and Son Limited, fat refiners of Grimsby, Lincolnshire, have devised a four part delivery/invoice set which has considerably reduced paperwork. With the new system the name and address of the customer and the completed order is written out by the salesman, instead of four times as was done previously. (see Figure 6.7)

When completed, the four part set is separated into delivery and invoice packs. The driver takes the delivery note and copy delivery note—parts 1 and 2 of the set—to the customer with the order. The delivery note is left with the customer and the copy delivery note is brought back to the office where it is checked against the invoice and copy invoice (parts 3 and 4) for changes to the original order. Part 3 is sent as an invoice, and no statement is sent unless requested. The invoice copy is filed in a weekly day book.

The invoice is priced, posted on to a machine, and sent to the customer. Gross profit margins on each order are entered in a special column on the copy invoice.

The copy delivery note is put into the customer's record file, and provides a readily available check on what the customer is purchasing, and the frequency of his purchases. The copy invoice with cash receipt is filed to form a weekly day book, from which costing and profit and loss accounts can be prepared.

Formerly, each salesman listed the customer's requirements on a sales record card. In the office, the order was transferred to a delivery sheet and copied into a duplicate delivery book by the driver of the vehicle in charge of the consignment. On completing the delivery the driver returned to the office with the delivery sheet signed by the customer. The office checked the delivery and order sheets for discrepancies and entered the actual goods delivered into a sales day book. An invoice was made out, priced and posted on to a hand-written multiposting board, and sent to the customer. Gross profit margins for each order (calculated from cost and selling prices) were entered into the day book. Statements for customers were written out at the month end.

With the new system, office staff has been reduced, through natural wastage, from three to one full time clerk, with part time help during busy periods.

The Pixie Pickles Company in Pendlebury has a similar system, also using a four part form which is completed at one writing, consisting of invoice and day book copy, and delivery note and office copy.

The delivery note and office copy are retained as a unit set and passed to the delivery driver who tears off the top copy and hands it to the customer. He returns the signed copy to the accounts department where the invoice and day book copy are priced. The invoice is immediately despatched to the customer and the day book copy is used for ledger posting. The unpriced office copy of the delivery note is used to update stock records and filed permanently (see Figure 6.9).

Another good example of an integrated set of forms is one used by the Randalls Group. When an order is received, details are entered on a set of forms comprising basic four documents:

1   Advice/receipt note
2   Invoice/stock control copy
3   Ledger copy
4   Branch copy

The only exception is when prices are calculated and added subsequently (see Figure 6.10).

The customer's name and address are entered in the box on the left of the form. If goods are taken over the counter, the advice note is signed by the customer.

The advice/receipt note, if not taken with the merchandise, is passed to stores for the order to be made up. It is then used to obtain the customer's signature on the receipt note portion on delivery.

The ledger copy and invoice/stock control copy meanwhile are passed to the office where prices are calculated and entered, stock details completed on the left of the form, and the address plate with the customer's name and address selected and printed through the two parts.

Six and seven part sets

Alexander, Fergusson and Company make out a set of six documents in one writing. These are:

1 Stock control copy
2 Delivery/receipt note
3 Day book (posting copy)
4 Invoice
5 Statistics/sales office copy
6 Copy invoice

Part 1, the stock control copy, is passed to stores for posting to stock records. The delivery receipt note is routed to the despatch bay; from here it accompanies the goods and, on delivery, the delivery section is left with the customer while the receipt signed by the customer is returned by the driver to the office. The day book copy is used for the day book, and is then filed.

Part 5 is used for notification to the sales department for analysis. When the receipt is returned to the office, the invoice is sent direct to the customer and the copy invoice put on permanent file. Figure 6.11 shows the invoice copy of the invoice used for stock cont:

Multitone Electric Company Limited complete seven forms in one writing, comprising two copies of the invoice, an advice note, a day book copy, a sales copy, a goods despatch copy with the top half perforated for use as a label, and a job card (see Figure 6.12). The job card is on staff manila stock for frequent handling in the works. The same form is also used for processing service and repair orders.

Documents for repair orders

There are many varieties of repair order retail outlets dealing in simple servicing work which simply need to give the customer a receipt for the goods left. Very often this contains little more than an order number for identifiying the goods, which are filed numerically. Some do not even contain the firm's name and address although, incredibly enough, the customer is often given a receipt with a copy of his own name and address.

A repair ticket should have at least the name of the firm as well as the address and telephone number. It is not unusual for a customer to discover a repair ticket some time later but to forget where the goods were left. It is advisable also to state when the goods will be ready and the customer's name so that a postcard may be sent if necessary to remind the customer that the goods are ready.

Figure 6.13 illustrates a simple repair order completed in three parts, one to accompany the article in the works, a receipt for the customer, and a control copy for either stores or accounts.

If instuctions are necessary, they should be written as precisely as possible and authorised by the customer. Wherever possible the final cost should be stated to avoid any needless delays and possible differences with the customer when the invoice is presented. Items which are to be charged or for which there is no charge under a service agreement or warranty should be clearly indicated before the customer is asked to agree on work to be carried out. The owner/manager should be able to provide a list of parts used and labour involved if asked to do so.

Ideally the invoice should be completed before the repair is collected to encourage immediate payment. The flow chart shown in Figure 6.14 illustrates how copies of repair order can be completed simultaneously for invoicing and accounting purposes.

Instructions are written on the three-part set and authorised by the customer at the very start. The first two parts are sent to the stores and the third to the works to serve both as an instruction sheet and as the worker's authority to obtain spares on presentation to the stores. It stays with the article until the job is completed, when it goes to the office.

On the issue of parts, the items and price are recorded on copies 1 and 2. A stock control sheet is entered at the same time. On completion of the job these two copies are sent to the office, where they are married up to copy 3 for costing and check for accuracy. Copy 1 is then used for sales analysis and filed, and copy 2 is used as an invoice which is posted to the customer or handed to him when he collects the repair.

Figures 6.15 and 6.16 show two examples of repair orders used in this type of system. Figure 6.17 is similar, except that the accounts copy is designed to serve as payment control.

Forms of customer index

A customers' index helps to avoid unnecessary questions being asked each time an order is placed and the delays this causes. This can consist of simple index strips containing such basic details as the name of each customer, address and delivery point, as shown in Figure 6.19.

Records on customers can also be designed to be used for developing sales and can serve as the basis of a mailing list. Past customers, even those who are satisfied, do not always return when they have new requirements. They may not know of the other types of goods which are available from the same sources. Prospective customers can be integrated in the index by using different coloured stock. Each card could include such information as:

1   Customer's business, trade or products
2   When a salesman last called
3   Names and positions of individuals seen by the sales staff or who have placed
     orders on behalf of the firm
4   Frequency of orders and the last time an order was placed
5   Occasions when quotations have been provided, indicating those resulted in
     an order.

Some firms maintain a complete history of sales, including special prices and discounts. This is all information indispensible to the sales staff.

In smaller firms, much of this information can be recorded on each customer's ledger card. This not only shows when a purchase was last made but gives the current standing of the account.

Figure 6.18 is a good example of a comprehensive record card for customers. The main insert card contains a summary of each month's sales. This information is provided by the override sheets on which are recorded each sales transaction. These sheets, which are thinner stock than the main cards, are divided into eight selling lines to provide statistics on sales. They are also used to indicate the selling lines which are not purchased by the customer and could be prompted.

The facing card is used to record enquiries from the customer and the quotations provided.

The visible edge makes provision for the name and address of the customer. The Jan to Dec scale is used for signalling either the month of the last order or the last call of the representative. Other signals are used to signify the lines the customer is buying.

Some sort of system must be introduced to identify customers with credit limit, and defaulters. In smaller firms this can be indicated by the ledger cards. Alternatively, the customers' index can be coded with labels and tabs to indicate those with credit facilities, credit limits, purchases in excess of which would require the approval of the owner/manager or the supervisor, and possibly the names of the individuals authorised to purchase on behalf of the firm.

It may be worth keeping a separate index of delinquent customers for quicker reference. This can take the form of simple card index strips similar to those shown in Figure 6.19 but giving the details of the amount owing, month of origin of the debt, and the amount of any payment made.

If for any reason it is not feasible to identify customers in this way, the customer's card from the credit customer's index can simply be withdrawn and any enquiries referred to the person who can explain to the customer why credit cannot be extended.

Uses of salesmen's reports

Properly designed sales reports can be used to indicate the efficiency of both individual salesmen and the sales force as a whole, through the number of calls made, the ratio of sales to calls, and so on. It is also possible to check whether each individual salesman is up to quota, which orders he did not get and the 'near misses' which may indicate a lack of preparation or training.

It is also important that any goods asked for by customers but which are not in stock are reported. This can be easily done by having sales people jot them down on special notepaper. Any successful substitutions should also be reported along with the original demand.

Dymo Limited of Feltham, Middlesex, use a system which combines both sales records and achievement reports. After each call the salesman takes the customer's sales record card from a tray, registers it over a weekly achievement report, and enters on both forms simultaneously details of goods required, sold, unavailable and so on (see Figure 6.20). The customer's name is added to the achievement report on the same line as the entry. At the end of the week the achievement report is totalled and the salesman sends copy to the regional sales manager.

On the back of the achievement report is a time-table on which each salesman enters his planned calls for the following week. The regional manager can then see where each salesman can be expected to be should it be necessary to contact him.

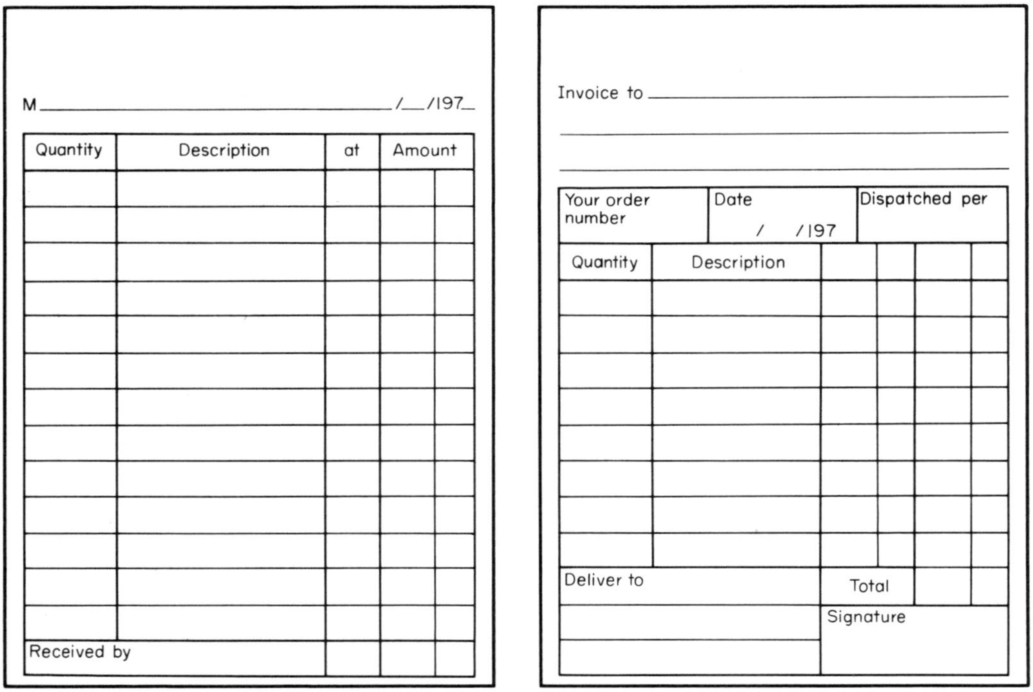

M ______ /__/197_

Quantity	Description	at	Amount
Received by			

Invoice to ______

Your order number	Date / /197	Dispatched per
Quantity	Description	
Deliver to	Total	
	Signature	

Figure 6.1 Two examples of standard sales slips.
These are standard continuous forms intended for use on Lamson Paragon registers. A copy of each slip is automatically filed in the register, which is locked, so that no sales slip can be left unaccounted for. Note that the space at the bottom of the form can be signed by the customer without having to turn the register around each time.

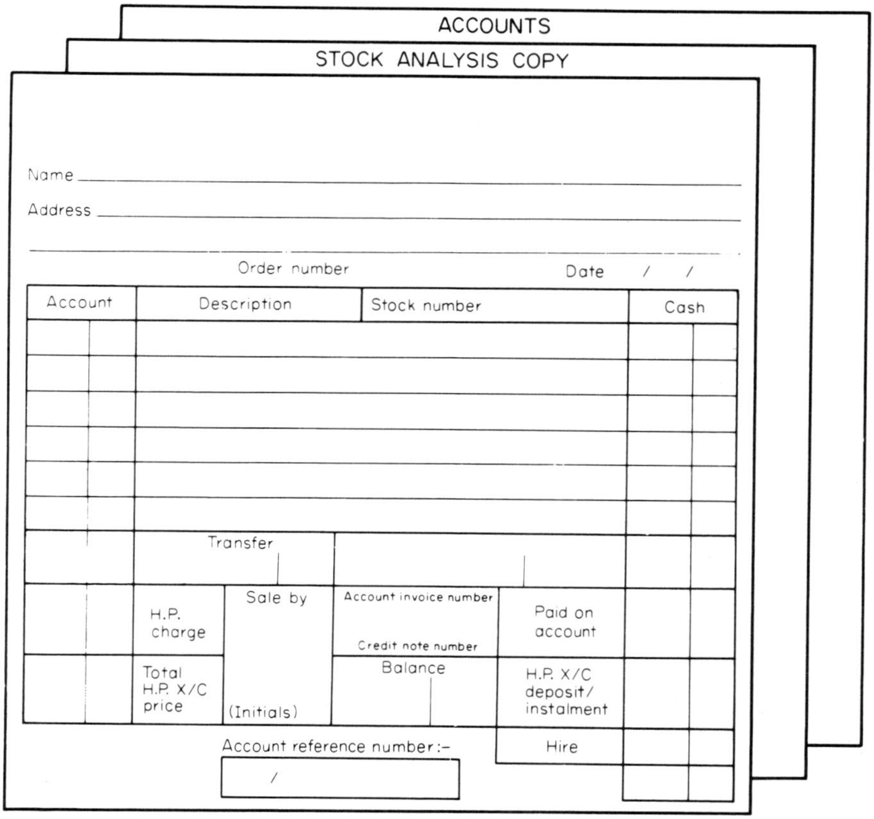

Figure 6.2 Sales slip.
A sales slip for use on a Paragon register with copies for stock control and accounts (Jones and Crossland Limited).

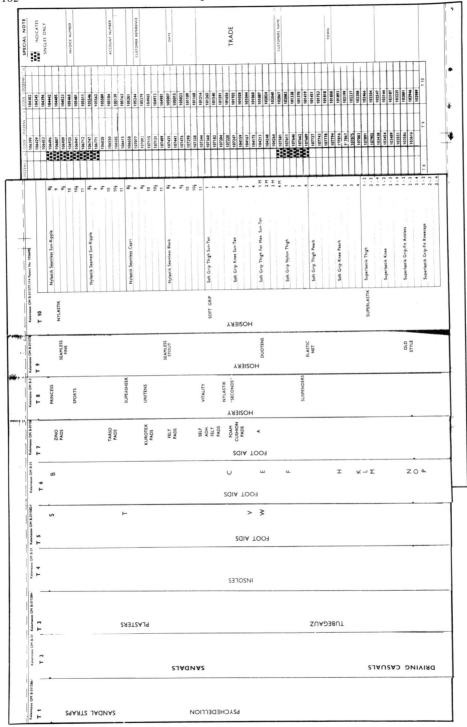

Figure 6.3   Sales order form (Scholl Limited).

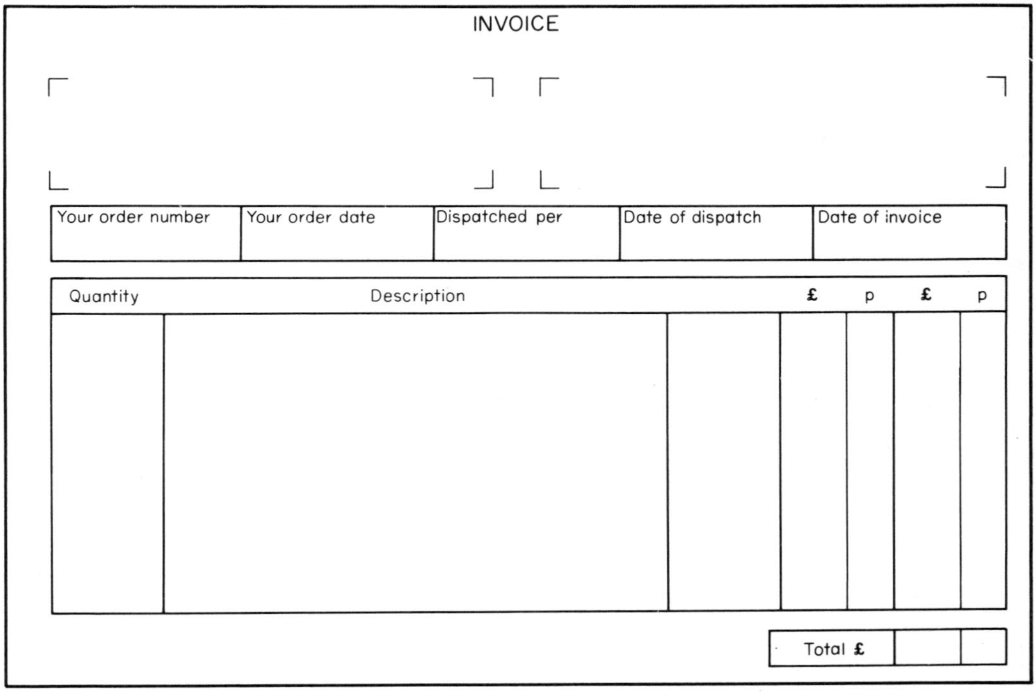

INVOICE

Your order number	Your order date	Dispatched per	Date of dispatch	Date of invoice

Quantity	Description		£	p	£	p

Total £

Figure 6.4 Standard invoice (Lamson Paragon).

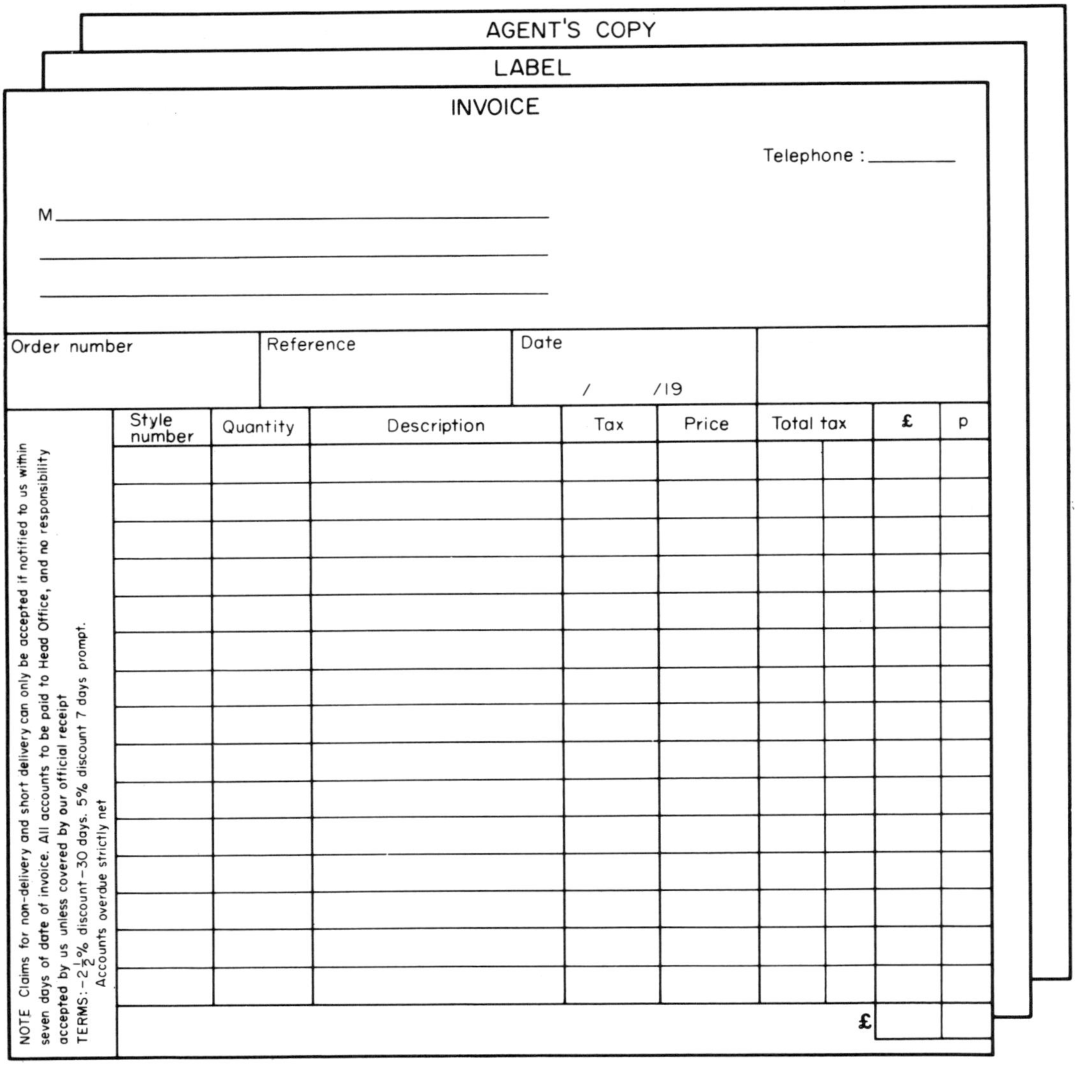

AGENT'S COPY									
LABEL									
INVOICE									

Telephone : _____

M_____

_____

_____

| Order number | Reference | Date | | | | | | | |
| | | / /19 | | | | | | | |

	Style number	Quantity	Description	Tax	Price	Total tax	£	p
						£		

NOTE Claims for non-delivery and short delivery can only be accepted if notified to us within seven days of date of invoice. All accounts to be paid to Head Office, and no responsibility accepted by us unless covered by our official receipt
TERMS:-2½% discount—30 days. 5% discount 7 days prompt.
Accounts overdue strictly net

Figure 6.5　Sales order form.
The top half of the second copy is perforated and used as a label for the delivery parcel (She-Type Limited).

AGENT'S COPY

OFFICE COPY

INVOICE

RECEIPT NOTE

Signature _____ Number of cartons

M

This is a priced copy
of your advice note

Order numbers	Quantity dozens	Representative	Dispatched per	Terms 2½% monthly	Date / /	Price per dozen	Date / /	£	p
		Brooms:		ADVICE NOTE					
		Bannisters:		A priced invoice which is a copy of this advice note will follow					
		Platforms:							
						Total			

Figure 6.6   Sales order form.
(Broom Manufacturing Company Limited).

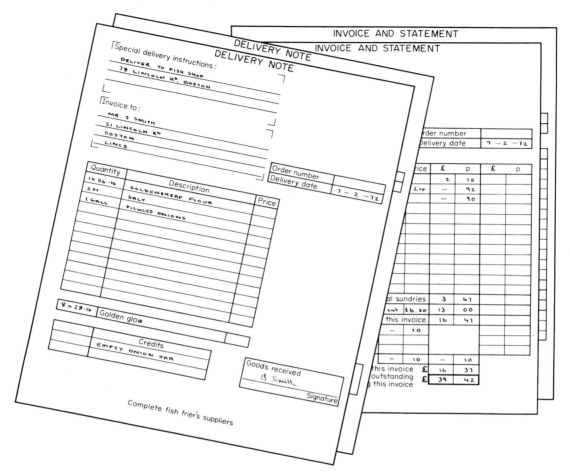

Figure 6.7   Invoice/delivery note.
The credit box is completed by the delivery van driver, who returns the second copy with the customer's signature to the office, where it is eventually filed under the customer's name as a full record of purchases. The blank space on the right hand side is available for the driver to enter any future order given to him. This would be recorded on a separate invoice. Parts 3 and 4, containing any changes from the original order, are also returned to the office, where they are priced and the gross profit worked out. The first price column is for sale prices and the second for cost prices (W Spray and Son).

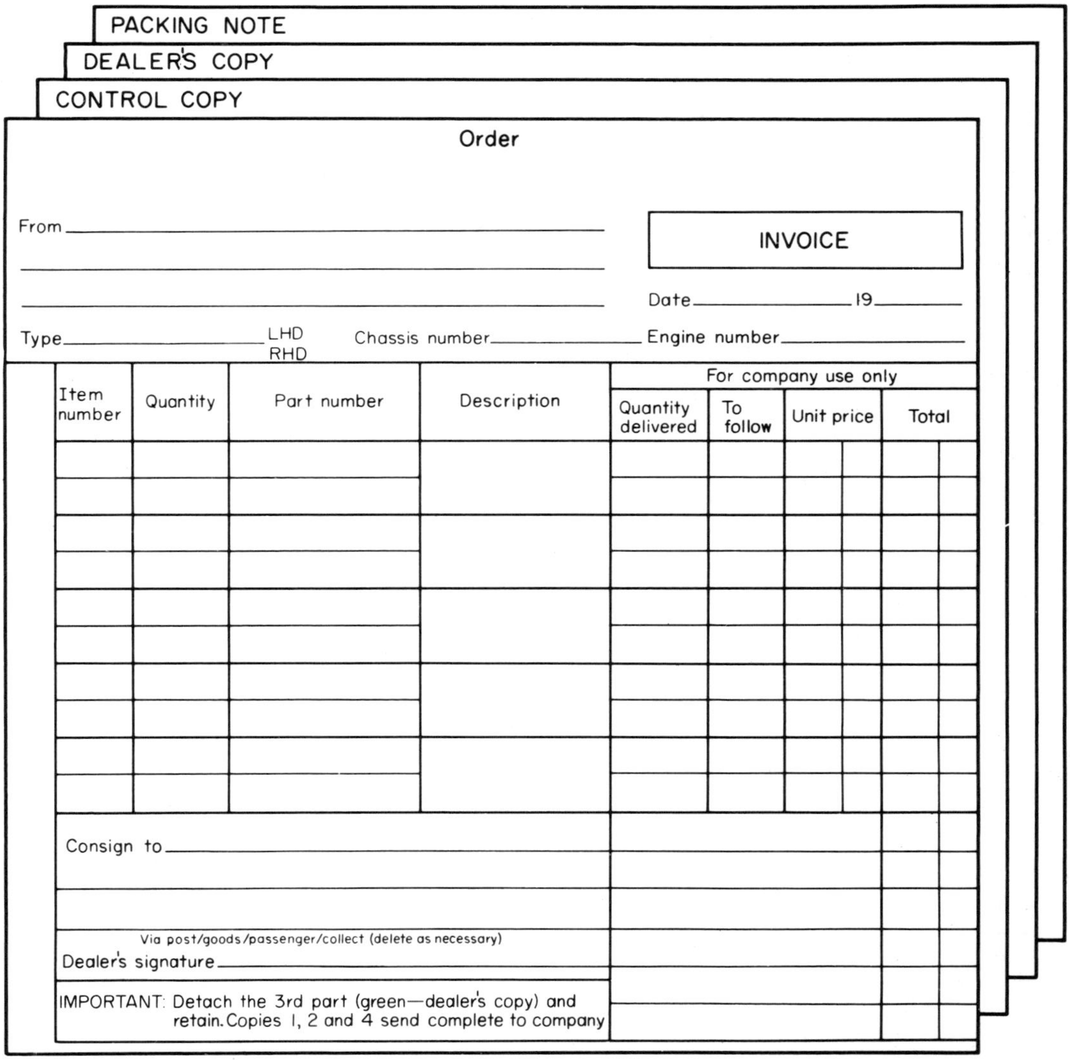

PACKING NOTE

DEALER'S COPY

CONTROL COPY

Order

From _____

_____

_____

| INVOICE |

Date _____ 19 _____

Type _____ LHD / RHD   Chassis number _____ Engine number _____

Item number	Quantity	Part number	Description	For company use only			
				Quantity delivered	To follow	Unit price	Total

Consign to _____

Via post/goods/passenger/collect (delete as necessary)

Dealer's signature _____

IMPORTANT: Detach the 3rd part (green—dealer's copy) and retain. Copies 1, 2 and 4 send complete to company

Figure 6.8   Four part order/invoice/despatch note.
(Thomas Wilcock & Son Limited).

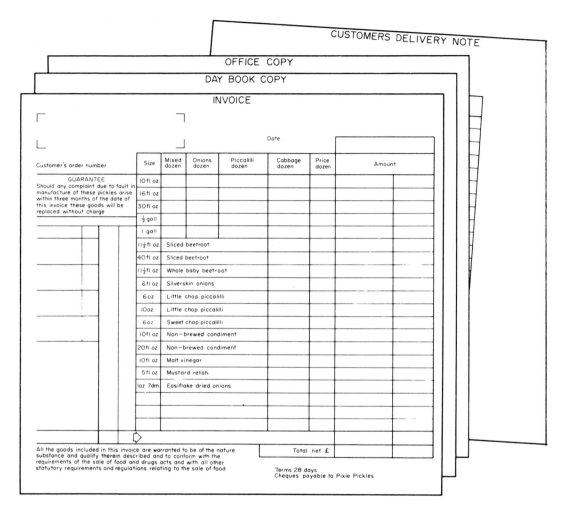

Figure 6.9   Four part order/delivery set.
(Pixie Pickles).

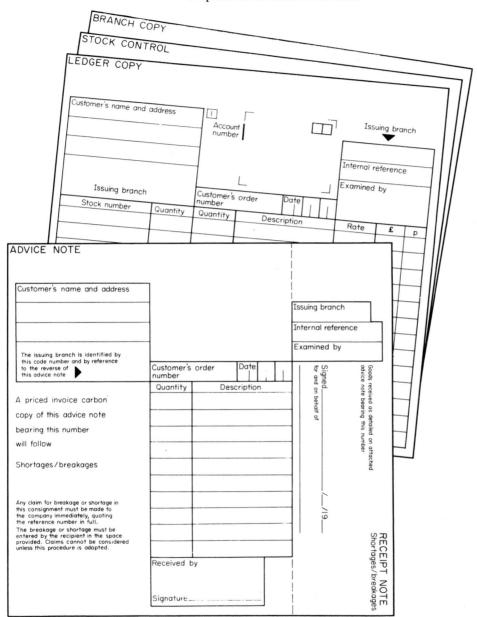

Figure 6.10   Invoice/delivery set.
This set of Lamson Paragon forms is used where goods are obtained over the counter or by prior order and despatch by Randalls' own transport. Where delivery is required, the advice note is used to serve as a delivery note, and in such cases only the receipt note portion is used (Randalls Group).

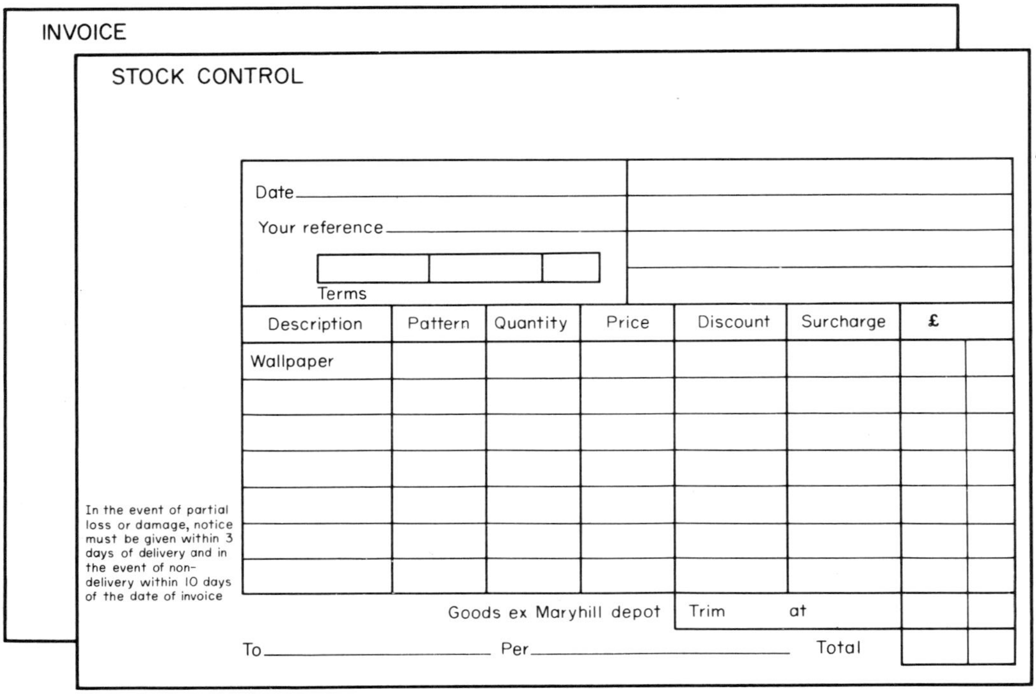

INVOICE								

STOCK CONTROL

Date_____

Your reference_____

Terms

Description	Pattern	Quantity	Price	Discount	Surcharge	£	
Wallpaper							

In the event of partial loss or damage, notice must be given within 3 days of delivery and in the event of non-delivery within 10 days of the date of invoice

Goods ex Maryhill depot   Trim   at

To_____ Per_____ Total

Figure 6.11   Invoice copy for stock control.
These are two forms of a six part set completed at one writing on a Paragon register. The prices appear on this copy but could be obliterated if necessary (Alexander, Fergusson and Company).

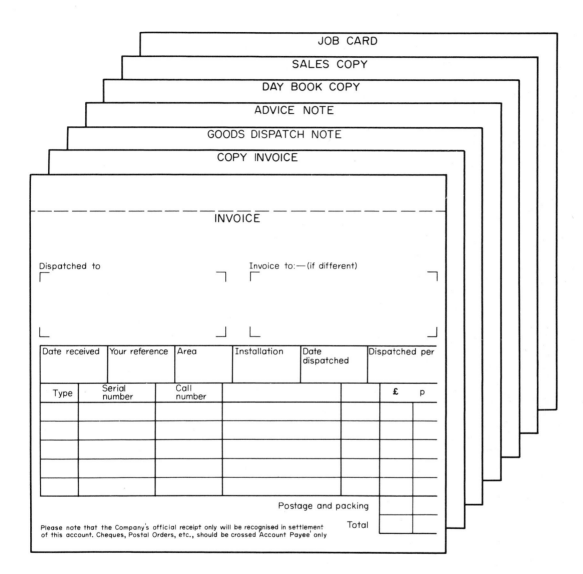

Figure 6.12   Seven part invoice set.
The top half of the goods dispatch note serves as a label for the parcel delivery or posting (Multitone Electric Company).

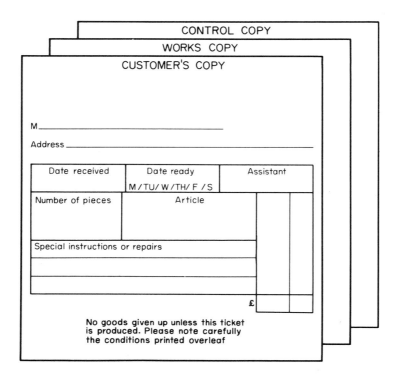

Figure 6.13   Repair order form.
A three part form, consisting of a works copy, customer's receipt, and a control copy for accounts or stores, completed in one writing on a Paragon register for continuous forms. Conditions of acceptance are printed on the reverse side of the customer's copy. The second copy is printed on manila stock for frequent handling.

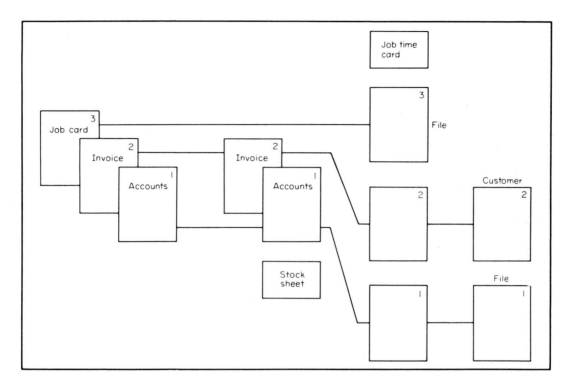

Figure 6.14   Repair work documents flow chart.
This simple flowchart summarises the distribution and functions of a three part set of dockets recommended by Lamson Paragon Limited. Additional copies can be included for such purposes as branch control, service manager or whoever is required to assess and load each day's work (Lamson Paragon).

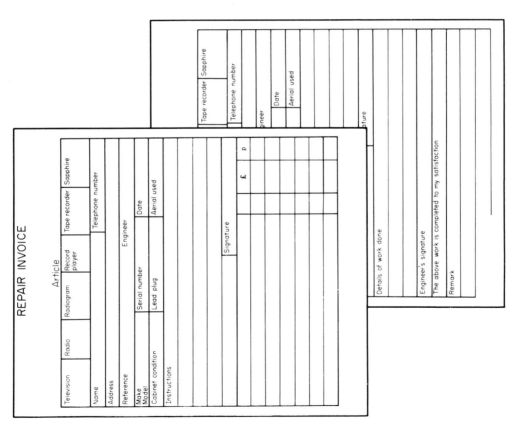

Figure 6.15   Repair order and invoice.
The standard form was designed by Lamson Paragon for use by firms dealing in electrical and similar types of appliances.

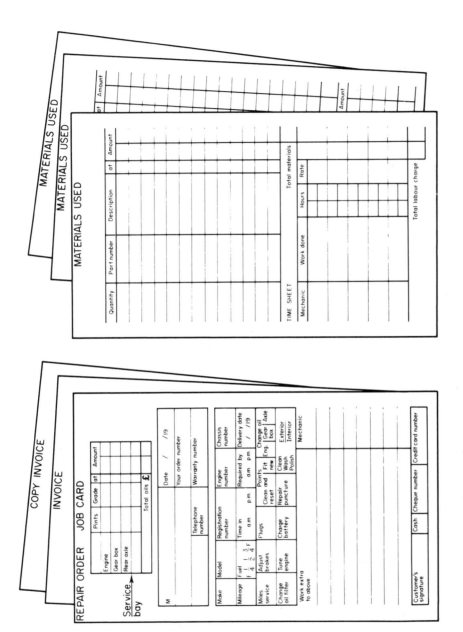

Figure 6.16.   This standard three part set was designed for garages and is used as continuous forms on a portable register.

The top half is duplicated on all three sheets but not the bottom part. The time sheet on the reverse side is for calculating service costs and is not used for payroll purposes, nor are details given on the invoice copy. The job card is printed on stiff manila stock to withstand continuous handling and adverse working conditions.

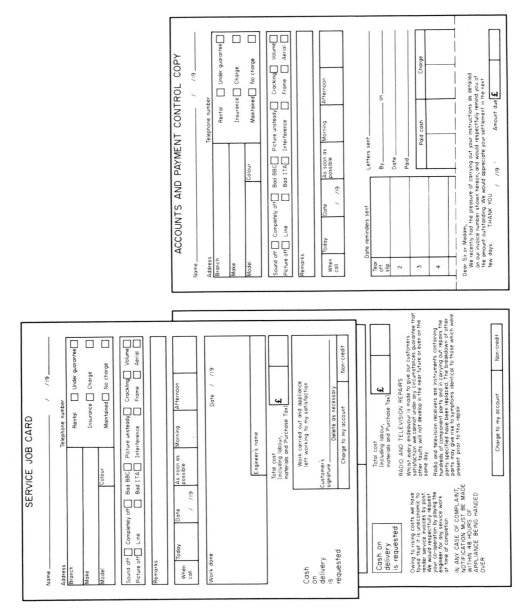

Figure 6.17   Repair order/account and payment control document.

Name		Address	

ENQUIRIES AND QUOTATIONS

Date	Description	Quotation number	Quantity	Price quoted	Follow up	Result

SALES

Date	Our order number	Customer order number	Quantity	Value	Quantity	Value	Quantity	Value	Quantity	Value	Quantity	Value	Quantity	Value	Total value

SALES SUMMARY IN £ p

Month	Quantity	Value	Quantity	Value	Quantity	Value	Quantity	Value	Quantity	Value	Quantity	Value	Quantity (Total)	Value (Total)
Jan														
Feb														
Mar														
Apl														
May														
June														
July														
Aug														
Sept														
Oct														
Nov														
Dec														
Total														

Name	Address											Lines buying							
Jan	Feb	Mar	April	May	June	July	Aug	Sept	Oct	Nov	Dec	1	2	3	4	5	6	7	8

Figure 6.18   Kardex sales control record (Remington Rand).

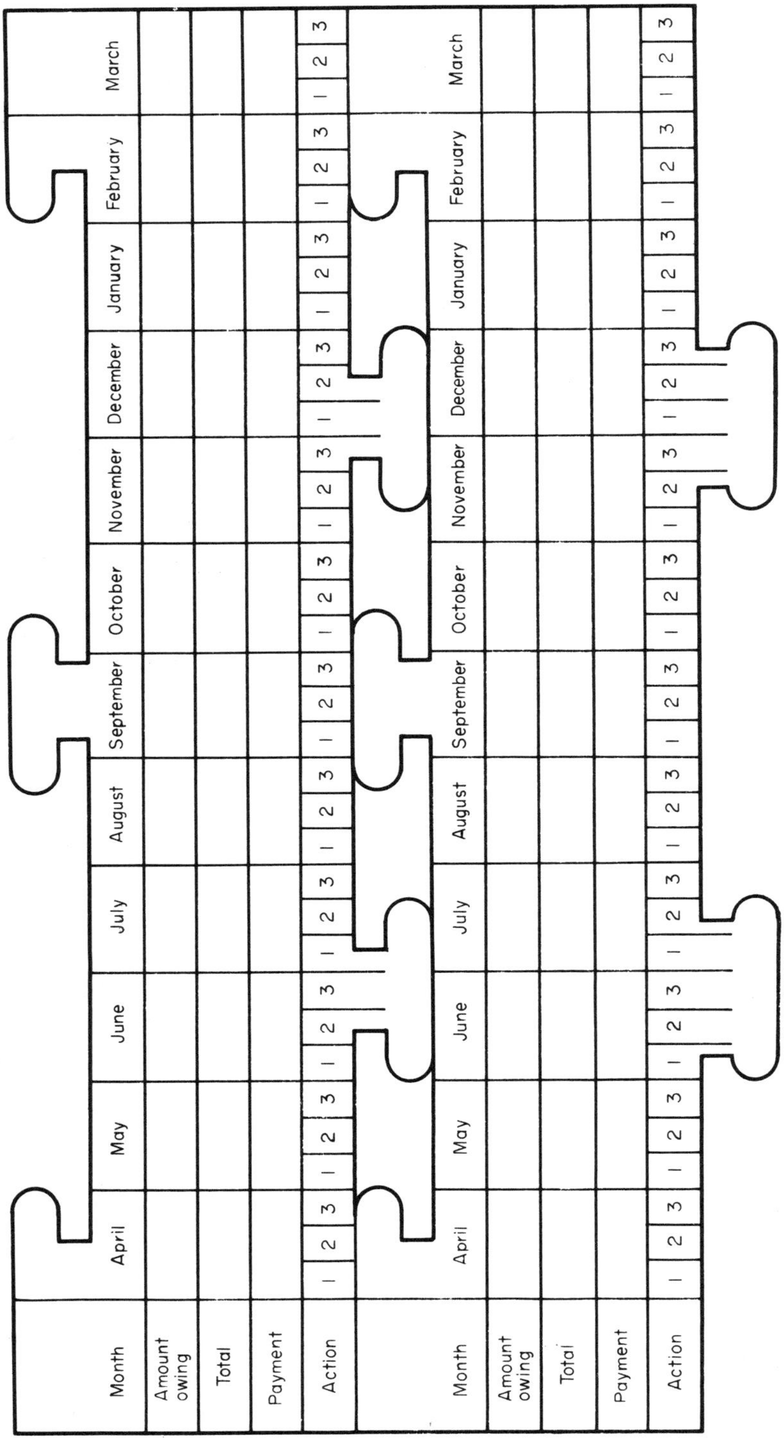

Figure 6.19   Credit control index.

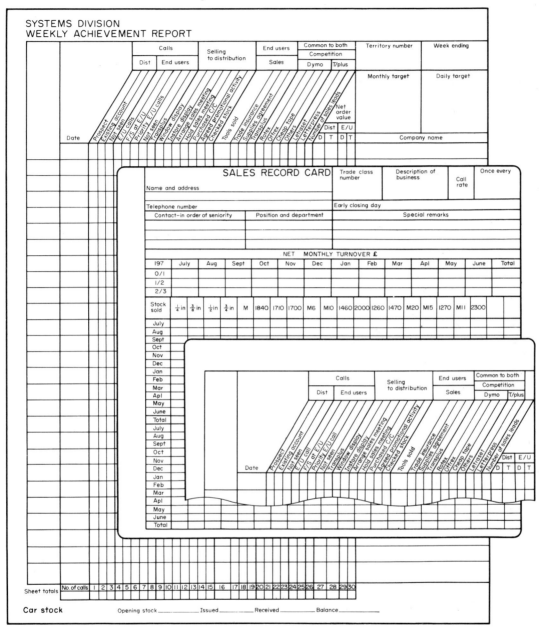

Figure 6.20 Customer's history record and weekly achievement report (Dymo Limited).

7

Personnel Records and Documents

It is essential that proper records be raised and maintained for every person in the employ of the company, not only to meet statutory obligations but in the employer's own interest—as well as the employee's. For this reason it is imperative that whoever is responsible for maintaining personnel records is informed at once of those engaged or leaving the firm and of any changes in status, transfers, or other relevant personnel information.

Form and value of personnel day book

Many companies maintain a day book or journal to record all employee movements as they occur. This type of journal, an example of which is illustrated in Figure 7.1, makes a valuable reference book and is particularly useful in firms with minimum forms. It is also useful when preparing other records and statistics. It can give a very quick picture of trends in labour turnover, for example.

The details to be recorded depend on the information needed. The 'new starters' section could include colums covering:

1 Actual data of starting
2 Reference of clock number
3 Name and sex
4 Age
5 Address
6 Job
7 Basic rate

The section dealing with terminations of employment could have columns detailing:

1 Personnel factors

2   Reason for terminationn
3   Length of service

Change of status form

In some companies· a single form is used for reporting any change in an employee's status, with the exception of termination. Usually a change of status form contains the nature of the change, the name and clock number of the employee concerned, the effective date of the change and, in the case of a transfer, the new clock number which is inserted by the office before the form is routed to anyone else concerned. Figure 7.2 is an example of a change of status form.

Forms of application for employment

The importance of a proper application form is not always understood and some organisations in fact dispense with the application forms altogether on the gounds of expense. This unfortunate attitude can lead to poor selection, and the need for greater training, as well as high labour turnover.

Basically, the application form should be designed to provide the information needed by the employer to decide on the applicant's eligbility and suitability for a vacancy.

In designing the form the whole range of jobs must be kept in mind. There is a wide variation between the information required from a prospective labourer and a skilled toolmaker and, on the staff side, between information required from a clerk, an industrial nurse and a senior executive. More details are usually required of staff who complete their forms at home and return them by post. Works application forms are normally completed either in the waiting room, immediately before the interview, or during the interview itself. Some firms have separate forms for young people and apprentices which devote greater space to school results, interests and ambitions and less space or none at all to previous jobs.

Examples of typical application forms are shown in Figures 7.3 and 7.4

There are two main types of application form. A comprehensive form covering the whole range of jobs can be designed, with sections reserved for particular applicants, such as young people, staff, women and so on. A note in bold print should advise others not to complete these sections. Alternatively, the application form can be designed in two parts, the first containing questions applicable to all prospective employees, the second varying for different applicants. The second part could be printed in another colour with the category of applicants for whom each form is intended prominent at the top of the form. This approach would reduce the amount of paper and avoid confusion among the various applicants.

Figures 7.5, 7.6 and 7.7 show good examples of this approach.

Contents of application forms

Every question included on an application form should help to screen, select or identify the candidate. Any other information, such as the applicant's religion, elementary education or the colour of his eyes, is questionable. It is also doubtful whether some information requested is really needed at this stage, or if it would be better obtained at an interview. Other information may not be required unless the applicant is accepted for employment and should not be asked for until that time.

Items on an application form broadly fall into two categories. The first comprises those which identify the candidate, such as name, address, and date of birth. It may be well to ask for both date of birth and age, incidentally; the age is more cenvenient to read but the date of birth is needed for personal records. This section can also include questions intended to elicit facts which might debar the applicant from employment, such as ill-health or age, or test the applicant's eligibility in accordance with company policy. These questions should be based on an analysis of the work to be done, and the characteristics of present employees successful in this work.

The second section is normally used to record the applicant's qualifications, education, experience and personal qualities. The section of the form headed *Previous Employment* is normally in reverse chronological order so that the applicant begins with his present or more recent job. If the interviewer wishes to go farther back into the applicant's history, the other details will not be out of sequence. A space for the candidate to cover any other points he feels relevant should be included on the form, especially on staff forms.

It is usual at the end of the form to add a statement, to be signed by the applicant, that the information given is a true and correct record. In some cases the statement continues with some such clause as: 'If accepted for employment I agree to abide by the terms and conditions laid down by the company'. It is also a good idea to have a section *For office use only* to record details of information which are required only if the applicant is engaged—such as his bank account number or National Insurance number, for example.

The format of the form should be structured so that the information required for each department, payroll for example, is together. It may even be practicable to include on the application form whole sections which would otherwise have to be maintained as separate forms, thus obviating the need for separate medical examination reports, engagement forms, and so on.

If the application form is intended to provide information for the employee's personal records, it should be designed to complement these to facilitate the transfer of data.

Forms for obtaining references

Just what value letters of reference are to a prospective employer remains a moot point.

The best approach is for the prospective employer to indicate to referees precisely the information sought.

Basically the employer should seek confirmation of statements made by the applicant and an objective appraisal of his personal character. A former employer, for example, should be asked to confirm employment dates, nature of duties and the reason for leaving. The referee should also be asked to state the capacity in which he has known the applicant and the length of time.

A number of firms send referees a standard reference as they indicate precisely the information required. At the same time, standard forms are useful in dissuading referees from making exaggerated comments and help to ensure a greater degree of accuracy and objectively in comparing candidates. Figure 7.8 is an example of a reference form.

Any such forms should be accompanied by a brief letter stating the purpose of the form and expressing appreciation. Alternatively, a standard letter can be printed on the form itself, possible with the questionnaire on the reverse side of the letter.

It should be stressed here that any reference given by one employer to another is intended to be treated in confidence and this should be stated in the request letter. References should not be filed with other personnel records, where they can be easily seen by clerks, but filed with other confidential documents.

Employees' income tax forms

A new employee arriving on his first day of work should be asked to hand over Parts 2 and 3 of certificate P45 and his National Insurance card, which he should have received from his previous employer. The P45 (Certificate of Particulars of Employee Leaving) will show the total earnings of the employee and the total amount of tax which has been deducted in the current income tax year and a code number representing the total value of the employee's allowances to be set against income tax liability.

The employer retains Part 2 of the P45 form and sends Part 3 to the tax office, where it is married up with Part 1. Before doing this, however, the employer should check the National Insurance number, shown as item 1 on the employee's P45, with the number on the National Insurance card to make sure that they do not differ. If they do, the National Insurance card number should be written above the number shown on Parts 2 and 3. Items 5 and 6 should also be checked to make sure that they agree, but these entries should not be altered. If there is any difference it should be reported to the tax office.

If the tax tables show a refund exceeding £20 is due to a new employee on his first day, the employer should enter the amount repayable in column 7 of the deduction card, complete form P47 and send it to the tax office. The refund should be made only on receipt of the authority from the tax office on form P48. Refunds of less than £20 may be paid immediately by the employer.

If a new employee is starting his first job, or has lost or is unwilling to produce parts 2 and 3 of his P45 for any reason—he may not wish to disclose his previous earnings, for instance—the new employer must complete Form P46 which is then sent to the tax office. He must then prepare a deduction card and deduct income tax from the employee's pay according to the emergency card tables until a code number has been notified by the tax office.

If a new employee claims that his previous employer has failed to provide a P45, a telephone call asking him to send it on may help to avoid the inconvenience to the worker of operating the emergency code. If the man has been unemployed it may be that the P45 which he presents to his new employer relates to an earlier tax year and the code may be out of date. The inspector should be asked to provide an up-to-date code and an emergency code should be used until this is received. However, where an emergency code would create hardship to the employee, it is better to telephone the Inspector's office and seek permission to operate the old code number until a new one is received.

A casual worker who claims that the Inland Revenue collect their tax from him directly should be asked to produce his direct payment card. Unless evidence of this is produced, the employee should be subject to the PAYE system. While it may be troublesome to do this, there is really no choice in the matter where wages are over £8 a week. The employer may be tempted to pay short term wages through 'petty cash' and attribute payments to other reasons, but this is technically incorrect and can lead to serious difficulties with the Inland Revenue.

Other initial documents

The new employee should be asked to produce his birth certificate (or passport) to verify his age for insurance and pension purposes. It may also be advisable to check his educational certificates and union membership cards. This is also a good time to obtain his signature for deductions from wages (see page 154).The appropriate entry should be made in the personnel journal or day book at this time.

Unless he received them at his selection interview the employee should receive some sort of handbook or sheet stating company employment practices and policies and any other publications on the company's products and uses. He should also be given at this time any instruction manuals necessary in his work, gate pass, identification badge or card, protective clothing, equipment, or other items necessary to his work.

The employee is normally asked to sign an issue form for such items and the form is then filed in his personal file, to be returned to him when employment is terminated or when the items are returned to the company. If any goods are not retruned the cost can be reclaimed in the same way as an ordinary debt, but it may not be deducted from his wages.

Medical certificates. In industries where a medical examination is required, it is important that a certificate is received for every new employee. This also holds true for new employees under the age of eighteen who, by law, cannot be employed for more than fourteen days without a certificate of fitness from an appointed factory doctor, who may require that the young person's school medical record be obtained from the local educational authority.

In issuing a certificate of fitness, incidentally, the doctor has the power to specify an interval after which re-examination is necessary, and it is unlawful to retain the young person without re-examination and a renewal of the certificate. Any conditions imposed by the factory doctor in his certificate may continue to be enforced until the young person reaches the age of eighteen. When no shorter interval is specified, all employees under the age of eighteen are required by law to receive a medical examination at least once a year.

Registration of private vehicles

If the number of vehicles that can park on company premises is limited, passes should be issued to employees and pass numbers recorded on personal files. Authorisation may be included on identification cards if these are also needed. Alternatively, car stickers can be provided for the windscreens or bumpers. This is a better method in that unauthorised cars are quickly shown up. If car parks are designated by particular departments or grades, different coloured stickers can be provided. The same colours can be used for the appropriate car park signs.

It may be necessary to have some form of registration or identification whereby the driver can be traced in his department in the shortest possible time in cases of damage, lights being left on, water or petrol leaking, and so on.

A card index system for vehicles can be very simply devised. Its sequence can be based either on the numerals or the letters of the car's registration number. All that is required is registration number, name and owner's department, and telephone extension at which he can be reached. The make and colour of the car could be recorded to prevent mistakes being made. A simple card of this nature could be made out every time a change of vehicle occurs, or a new employee enters the firm, to ensure the index is kept up-to-date.

Form and contents of personal records

It is important to keep records for every employee which can serve as a central reference point for any information required about personnel. In some firms these records are kept separate from any other documents. In other firms an employee's record is printed on a filing folder or on a large envelope in which can be placed all other documents concerning the employee.

Sometimes the application form is printed on heavy stock to serve as the employee's personal history record. In this way little of the information on it needs to be transferred to other documents, thus avoiding the chance of errors creeping in.

Design and format.   The layout of an application form intended to serve as a personal record should be specifically designed to fulfil this function. The applicant's name and other identification should be at the top of the form, for example, to facilitate retrieval from the files.

In general the contents of personal records cards should be divided into specific fields. In some firms the information is separated according to its use by various departments. At least one firm distinguishes between information obtained from the applicant, additional information gathered during his employement and information about former employees acquired after termination.

It is helpful to design the record card so that all permanent information is separate from the other items which are likely to change, such as addresses. In some firms information subject to change is written on the record in pencil or adhesive labels which can be removed. A record of changes in status, education or wage rates may be a relevant part of the employee's history, however; it is better to allow sufficient space for the amendment of such items with a new line stating the up-to-date position every time there is a change in any one particular. This gives the current positions and the history at a glance. In those industries where wages are related to the cost of living index, a separate wage book is usually kept, as it would be impossible to amend all the cards for every minor change.

Nature of contents

A personal history record may contain any of the following:

Surname	Forename	Identification number
Business address		
Residence		
Home telephone		
Sex M/F	Marital status	
Name of spouse	Number of children	
Date of birth	Place of birth	Nationality
Date commenced employment		
Contact in emergency:	Name	
	Address	
	Place of employment	
	Relationship	
Medical restrictions	Physically disabled register	
Physical examinations		
Employee grade or group		
Union code		
In-company location code		
Department, group, section		
Payroll number	Tax code	
Major accidents		
Bank/giro account number		
Parking lot number		
Gate pass number		

Job classification code		
Termination	Type	Date
Retirement		Date
Security clearance		

Non-essential information which may nevertheless be useful could include:

Professional associations		
Examinations completed		
Educational achievements		
Languages	Proficiency	
Military service		
Military training		
Skills	Type	Experience
Management experience		
Test scores		
Union membership		
Previous employment		

Personal history cards can also be used to record the employee's work performance, achievements both in his work and socially, as well as accidents and absences. Examples of personal history record cards are shown in Figures 7.9, 7.10 and 7.11.

Filing of personal records

Personal records are best filed in straight alphabetical order, although in some firms records of trainees, those worthy of promotion, and so on are filed separately. The division of the file into too many sections leads to confustion and wasted time searching, however, and it is far better to flag individual cards filed in straight alphabetical order.

Accident reports

An accident report should be completed as soon as possible after every accident, before memory fades. Normally, the immediate line supervisor originates the report, though some of the personal details may have to be completed in the office.

Reports of accidents are needed by various individuals and authorities, in addition to the HM Factory Inspector and the Ministry of Social Security.

Management need the information to investigate the cause of each particular accident and to take steps to avoid similar accidents. Periodic analyses of accidents may show a pattern which might require changes in working arrangements.

The insurance company with which the firm insures against common law liability may have to be informed. The doctor treating the employee may need to be given some information. The safety committee of the firm will also expect details.

The details required by these different bodies varies. It is therefore advisable to have an accident report form which is comprehensive.

The questions most frequently asked on an accident form are:

1   Name, clock number, sex, age, occupation
2   Address, married or single, children under sixteen, weekly earning (completed by the personnel or wages officer if employee loses time)
3   Date and time of accident
4   Date and time accident reported
5   Date and time injured employee stopped work as a result of accident
6   Time he started work on day or night of accident
7   Number of hours of continuous employment before accident
8   Cause of accident
9   What exactly was employee doing at the time (in detail)
10 Was he authorised or permitted to do what he was doing?
11 If the accident was due to machinery state:
 (a) Name of machine and part causing accident
 (b) Whether in motion by mechanical power at the time of accident
12 Nature and extent of injury, stating exact part of body affected
13 State whether employee received treatment at:
 (a) First-aid box (state which)
 (b) Ambulance room
 (c) Hospital (state which)
 (d) Own doctor (state name)
14 Name and clock number(s) of any person(s) who witnessed the accident
15 Was personal protective clothing or equipment necessary for the work being done at the time of the accident. If so:
 (a) Was it provided?
 (b) Was it being used?
16 Written statements from witnesses are often requested on the accident form and space is allowed for observations and other relevant information.
17 An office section checklist is sometimes includedd covering:
 (a) Form 43 sent to Factory Inspector
 (b) Entry in accident book checked
18 Entry in general register (Form 31a) recorded
19 Ministry of Social Security claim form received
20 Employer's liability insurance form sent
21 Reported to accident prevention committee
22 Date employee returned to work
23 Number of days lost
24 Any disablement on return

Some firms have a section for recommendations on action to be taken to avoid similar accidents. It is advantageous to consult workers and ask their advice about any proposed changes. Figure 7.12 shows an example of an accident report form.

Medical records

Many firms, particularly those with a full time or visiting medical officer or nurse, keep individulal medical records for all employees. In other firms, a record is raised only when an employee sees the medical officer for the first time. Figure 7.13 shows an example of a medical record. How complete such records should be must, of course, depend on the objectives of the medical department and the type of work involved.

The medical history should have two parts: the confidential information completed by and available to the medical officer and nurse only, and routine information which can be completed by a clerk.

The office should be notified of any visits by an employee to the first aid or medical section or to the company doctor. In smaller firms, and where treatment is usually given by first aiders at the place of work, this can be done by a simple system of notes originated by the supervisor. Duplicate tear-off sheets are probably the most satisfactory type of form because the duplicates can be despatched daily. Otherwise, the information may be received only sporadically—for example, when a page is completed.

Where there is medical section or company nurse, the note is taken by the employee to the nurse who keeps the main portion. A perforated section may be returned to the supervisor or the office for their information or given to the employee to remind him of another appointment.

The medical section of a company normally keeps a day book in which are recorded the following details:

1   Date
2   Time
3   Name
4   Sex
5   Department and number
6   Reason for attendance
7   Details of treatment

The day book may be a bound register or a loose leaf binder. It may have tear-off duplicate pages if a copy is needed for inspection by the medical officer. Where it is agreed that the day book is available for information to management, it will be for the doctor or the staff of the medical department to decide which information is confidential and should be recorded separately.

Forms relating to termination of employment

When an employee leaves a job for any reason, the employer should complete a form

P45 showing the total earnings in the current income tax year to the date of leaving and the total amount of tax which has been deducted.

Part 1 of the form is sent by the employer immediately to the Inspector of Taxes and Parts 2 and 3 are handed to the departing employee who may also be given a blank form P50 if it is known that he is not taking up new employment. Form P50 is required by the employee to claim refund of tax which may be due to him should he become temporarily or permanently unemployed. If the employee has died, a D is entered in a box indicated on the form and all three parts are sent to the tax office. In the case of an employee still affected by a Garnishee Order or an Attachment of Earning Order who ceases employment for any reason, the employer must notify the appropriate officer of the court that made the order.

Forms of notice.   Most firms require that notice of termination of employment given by either side should be in writing. A standard letter can be used by the employer both for himself and for the employee to sign.

Under the Contracts of Employment Act the employee is required to give his employer at least one week's notice if he has been with him continuously for twenty six weeks or more. This does not increase with longer service, although a contract may require a longer period of notice.

Employees are entitled to a minimum one week's notice after thirteen weeks, six weeks after ten years' service and eight weeks after fifteen years.

The Industrial Relations Act, incidentally, makes it illegal for an employer to dismiss an employee without good reason. Where the employee claims he has been unfairly dismissed, it is for the employer to show the reason for dismissal.

Calculation of redundancy payment

When employment is terminated because of redundancy the employer is obligated to make a redundancy payment to the employees who qualify. To qualify for a redundancy payment an employee must have normally worked for twenty-one hours or more a week, have completed a minimum of 104 weeks' continuous service with the present employer, and be between the ages of eighteen and sixty-five (or sixty for women).

According to the Redundancy Payments Act, the redundancy payment must be made immediately upon termination of employment, the amount depending on age and years of service, as follows:

1   For each complete year of service after forty-first birthday, 1½ week's pay
2   For each complete year of service, apart from those covered by 1, after twenty-second birthday, 1 week's pay
3   For each complete year's service, apart from those covered by 1 and 2, after eighteenth birthday, ½ week's pay

Reckonable service is limited to the twenty years prior to redundancy. Calculation of a week's pay for all employees is the same as that under the Contracts of Employment; only for shiftworkers does a different calculation apply. Payments are calculated on a maximum wage of £40 a week. Any earnings above this amount are not taken into account. The maximum payment under the scheme is therefore £1200.

Redundancy payment rebates

The employer may claim a rebate for redundancy payments from a fund to which he has contributed no later than six months after the date of termination of the employment, unless the matter has been deferred to a tribunal within this period. Form RP3 must be completed and sent to the local Employment Exchange, unless the redundancy payment is being reduced because of pension, in which case a special form must be used.

The claim must be made in writing and must include the date on which the employment terminated and the method by which the amount of the employer's payment has been calculated. Form RP2 must be used for claiming rebate from the redundancy fund. Notice must be given not less than fourteen days before the date on which the termination of employment is to, or is expected to, take effect.

Where the contracts of ten or more employees are to terminate on the same date or within a period of six days, prior notice of at least twenty-one is required by law. Form RP1 should then be sent to the local Employment Exchange.

If the information required involves a calculation which is not practicable for the employer to make in time to include it in the written notice, he must indicate that it will follow later. The missing information must be delivered as soon as practicable to the same local office as that to which the notice is delivered. If any of the required information is not known or not completely known to the employer, that fact must be stated.

Offer of alternative work.　　If an employee unreasonably refuses an offer, either of a renewal of his contract of employment to take effect immediately or of suitable alternative employment, either with the same firm or with a subsidiary or parent company, he is not entitled to a redundancy payment. The offer must be made to the employee before the due date of termination of the new job and the alternative employment must start within four weeks.

The offer must be made in writing. It should contain enough particulars to give a clear idea of what is being offered—what the work is, where it is, rates of pay and any other terms and conditions that are different from those under which the employee has been working up to then. Figure 7.14 gives an example of a form for use as a written statement offering redundant employees alternative work. These signed statements should be filed with the employee's personal records to protect the employer from any future claim for redundancy pay.

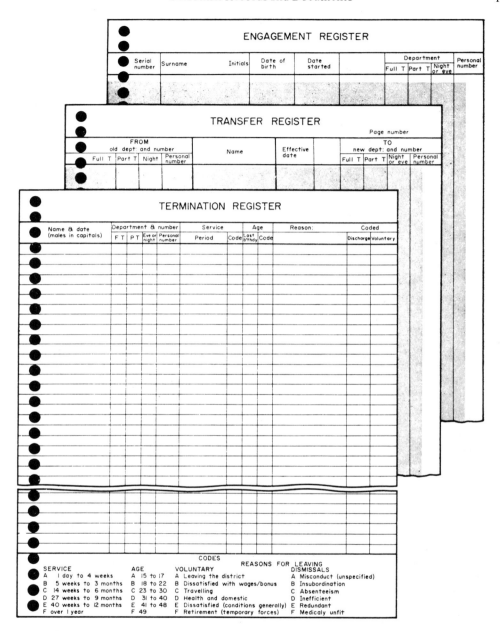

Figure 7.1 **Personnel journal or day book.**

These standard sheets are of toughened paper to withstand regular use and perforated to go into a multiple ring binder. The serial number on the engagement register is continuous and thus indicates the number of movements over any period. Department numbers and employee personal numbers, allotted in the categories men, full-time women, part-time women, are used to show movements that have taken place either in a department or in a main category of employee.

Confidential   Please complete in block capitals. Delete sections not applicable

To Group Personnel Services   Please note the following amendment(s) and take the necessary action

Clock number

Name Mr / Mrs / Miss _____

Department/company

Job title _____

Cost centre

1   New employee (GPS use only)

Date of starting	Hours of work	Date of birth	Rate of pay	Per	Bonus/ merit	Per
				Year Week Hour		Year Week Hour

National Insurance card received and number			P45 received	

2   Transfer

Date of transfer	Department/cost centre		New job title
	From	To	

Is there a change in pay and/or status?   Yes/No
If Yes complete section 3 below

3   Wage/ salary/ status/ change

Date effective	Present rate	New rate	Regrading	
			From	To

4   Termination

Date of leaving	Leaving code	Holiday days outstanding (staff only)	Would you re-employ?
			Yes/No

Authorisation

_____ Manager   _____ Date

_____ Divisional Head (where applicable)   _____ Group Personnel Services

Figure 7.2   Personnel data amendment form (Twinlock Group).

APPLICATION FOR EMPLOYMENT

Surname			Forenames		

Date of birth		Height	Married/single/widowed	Nationality

| Date of birth of children | Boys | | | |
| | Girls | | | |

Address	Telephone No

Health (mention any disability, serious illness or operation which you have had)

Are you prepared to undergo a medical examination?	Name and address of Doctor	Are you a registered disabled person
Have you been previously employed or refused employment by this company?	Are you related to, or do you know anyone in our employ?	No of certificate if registered

Next of kin
(Name and address)

Position now desired	Salary expected	Notice required by present employer

SCHOOL RECORD

Names of schools attended	Dates	Scholarships won, examinations passed with subjects taken	Dates

FURTHER EDUCATION

University, technical college, evening classes, institutes, etc	Courses or subjects studied	Diplomas, certificates, etc	Dates

School/college offices held, part taken in games, societies, other activities

Figure 7.3   Application form.
This is the first page of a four-page application form. The remaining pages cover positions held, references, foreign languages, spare-time activities, space for additional information from the applicant, interview notes and conditions of employment.

Surname	Position applying for
Mr	
Mrs	
Miss	

| Other names | How did you hear of us? |
| | Give name of newspaper, etc |

Address	Date of birth	Place of birth
	Nationality	Marital status
Telephone number		

| Name and address of next of kin | Forenames and dates of birth of children under nine years of age | | | |
| Telephone number | Is there someone to mind the children? |

| Names of friends or relatives with company | |

| If you have previously had employment with the company, give name of department, dates and reason for leaving | |

| Disabilities (if any) | Registration number |

Have you ever suffered from

        Chest complaints?   When?

        Dermatitis?   When?

        Diabetes?   When?

        Epilepsy?   When?

        Have you ever received compensation under the
        Industrial Injuries Acts?

        Have you ever had any serious illness (other than
        those mentioned above) or operation?

Figure 7.4   Application form.

EDUCATION			
Secondary, public or grammar school	From	To	Details of exam results
Further education (Day or evening technical college, postal course, etc)	From	To	Details of exam results, courses taken or being taken

Details of apprenticeship or training received

Have you any other skills or abilities which might interest us? (eg Foreign languages, mechanical aptitude, etc)

Membership of professional bodies, unions, etc

PREVIOUS EMPLOYMENT				
Name and address of present or last employer	Job	Rates/wages	Dates	

Dates of service in HM forces—from   to

Branch or regiment   Trade   Last rank

It is understood that you may apply for references from my present and previous employers, prior to engagement	Signed _____
It is also understood that, should I take up employment with the company, wages are paid on Fridays for work completed the previous Friday	Date _____

Personnel department use only
Interviewed by
Remarks

Figure 7.4   continued

```
Application for employment as _____

I PERSONAL PARTICULARS _____

Surname _____

Forenames _____

Present address _____

_____

Permanent address (if different) _____

_____

Telephone number _____   Date of birth _____

Nationality _____   Marital status _____

Number, age and sex of children _____

Name of next of kin _____   Relationship _____

Address _____

_____

Occupation _____

Health  Have you ever suffered from any serious disease or disability ? If so please give details  (Give

RDP number if appropriate) _____

_____

_____

Hobbies or leisure pursuits _____


2 EDUCATION

Name and type of secondary schools attended

_____ From _____ to _____

_____ From _____ to _____

_____ From _____ to _____

Examinations passed (please give details) _____

_____

_____
```

Figure 7.5   Application form for staff (Richard Costain Limited)

This form is used in connection with all weekly and monthly paid staff irrespective of level.

Further education colleges and universities attended

_____ From _____ to _____

_____ From _____ to _____

Examinations passed (for degrees, please give subject and details) _____

_____

Professional qualifications _____

_____

_____

Knowledge and standard of foreign languages spoken _____

3 EMPLOYMENT RECORD

Employment record, including service in HM Forces, commencing with present employer
(please use separate sheet of paper if necessary)

Name and address _____

_____

Date, salary and job title on joining _____

Current salary _____ Length of notice required _____

Present job title _____

Reason for wishing to leave _____

Name and address _____

_____

Date, salary and job title (a) on joining _____

(b) on leaving _____

Reason for leaving _____

Figure 7.5   continued

Name and address _____

_____

Date, salary and job title (*a*) on joining _____

(*b*) on leaving _____

Reason for leaving _____

Name and address _____

_____

Date, salary and job title (*a*) on joining _____

(*b*) on leaving _____

Reason for leaving _____

Name and address _____

_____

Date, salary and job title (*a*) on joining _____

(*b*) on leaving _____

Reason for leaving _____

Please list all training courses attended of over one week's duration including details of any apprenticeships served

Please give full postal addresses of 3 persons or companies to whom reference may be made (Business references preferred)
NB your present employers will not be approached without your permission

Name and address _____

_____

Name and address _____

_____

Name and address _____

_____

Figure 7.5   continued

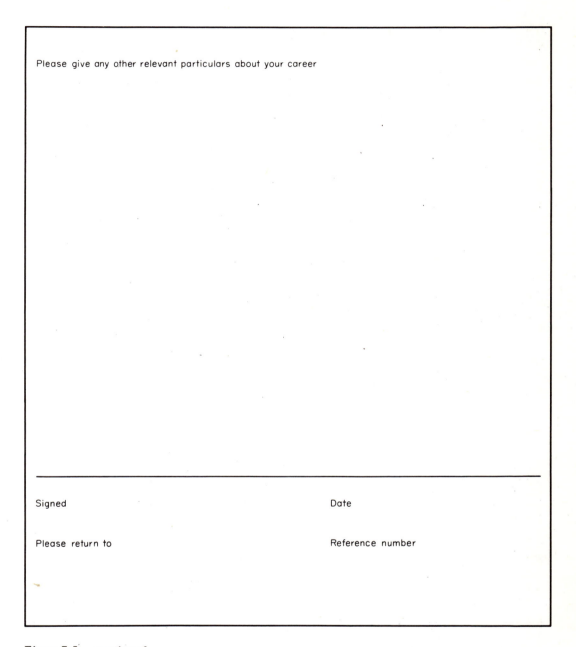

Please give any other relevant particulars about your career

Signed   Date

Please return to   Reference number

Figure 7.5   continued

---

3 EMPLOYMENT RECORD

If applying for secretary/typist position give your current speed

Shorthand _____ words per minute   Typing _____ words per minute

If applying for machine operator position, state types of machine and length of experience

_____

Employment record commencing with present employer. Two or more previous employers will be asked to give references, but your present employer will not be approached without your permission

Name and address _____

_____

Current salary (including bonus and luncheon vouchers) and position _____

_____ Notice required _____

Name and address _____

_____

Date, salary and position on joining and leaving _____

_____

Name and address _____

_____

Date, salary and position on joining and leaving _____

_____

Name and address _____

_____

Date, salary and position on joining and leaving _____

_____

Signed _____   Date _____

Please return to   Reference number

For office use only			
Position	Commencing salary	Date started	Source of recruitment

---

Figure 7.6   Application form for female staff (Richard Costain Limited).

Application for training as _____

I PERSONAL PARTICULARS

Surname _____

First names _____

Present address _____

_____

Permanent address (if different)_____

_____

Telephone number_____   Date of birth_____

Nationality _____   Marital status _____

Name of next of kin _____   Relationship _____

Address _____

_____

Occupation _____

Health. *Have you ever suffered from any serious disease or disability? If so please give details*

_____

_____

Interests. *Please give any information about yourself which you feel would be relevant to your application. Include details of any vacation work*

Figure 7.7   Application form for trainees (Richard Costain Limited).

2 EDUCATION

Please list name and type of schools, colleges or universities attended

_____ From _____ to _____

_____ From _____ to _____

_____ From _____ to _____

_____ From _____ to _____

Examinations taken Please list subjects taken, dates, examining body, results and grades obtained

Examinations to be taken

Please give full postal addresses of 2 persons to whom references may be made (One should be your housemaster or headmaster)

Name and address _____

_____

Name and address _____

_____

Signed _____ Date _____

Please return to _____ Reference number _____

Figure 7.7 **continued**

Dear Sir,

    The above-named has applied to this company for employment as a _____

and states having been in your service as _____ from _____

to _____ Clock number was _____

    We shall be greatly obliged if you will kindly confirm this and answer the questions detailed over, concerning the applicant. A stamped addressed envelope is enclosed for your reply which will be treated in strict confidence.

                                   Yours faithfully,

When did applicant enter your employment ?	
When did applicant leave your employment ?	
Was employment continuous during this period ?	
Reason for leaving ?	
In what capacity was applicant employed by you ?	
At what salary or wage ?	

Has applicant given satisfaction in the following:
     (a) Conduct
     (b) Honesty
     (c) Workmanship
     (d) Timekeeping
     (e) Sobriety	

Was general health good ?	
Did applicant receive any injury while in your employ ? If so, please state nature of accident	
Has applicant at any time received, or is applicant at present in receipt of, compensation ?	
Is applicant to your knowledge registered under Disabled Persons (Employment) Act ?	
Did you receive a reference with this person ? If so, from whom?	

General remarks :

Date _____

Signature _____

Designation _____

Figure 7.8   Reference form.

Name			Date of joining	
Nationality	Remuneration		Date of leaving	
	Date	Amount	Reason	
Date of birth				
Marital status				
Number of children at time of joining			Region/division	
Qualifications			Permanent transfers	
			Date	Region
Languages (fluent)				
			Promotions	
			Date	Position

Experience prior to joining ABC Limited			
Date		Position	Company
From	To		
Periods of illness (over 2 weeks)			
Date		Nature of illness	
From	To		

Figure 7.9   Personal history record.

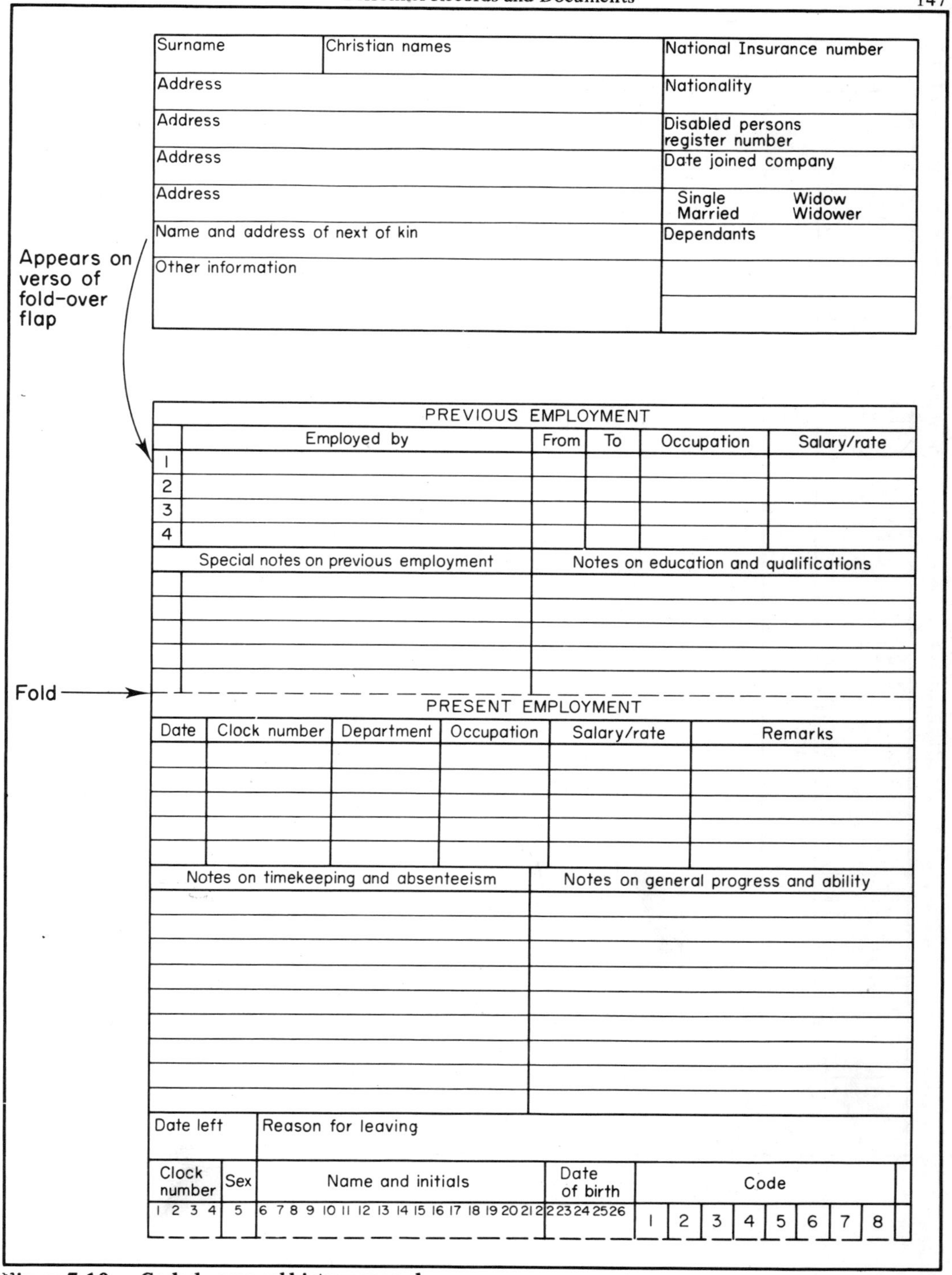

Surname	Christian names	National Insurance number
Address		Nationality
Address		Disabled persons register number
Address		Date joined company
Address		Single Widow Married Widower
Name and address of next of kin		Dependants
Other information		

Appears on verso of fold-over flap

PREVIOUS EMPLOYMENT

	Employed by	From	To	Occupation	Salary/rate
1					
2					
3					
4					

Special notes on previous employment	Notes on education and qualifications

Fold →

PRESENT EMPLOYMENT

Date	Clock number	Department	Occupation	Salary/rate	Remarks

Notes on timekeeping and absenteeism	Notes on general progress and ability

Date left	Reason for leaving

Clock number	Sex	Name and initials	Date of birth	Code
1 2 3 4	5	6 7 8 9 10 11 12 13 14 15 16 17 18 19 20 21 22	23 24 25 26	1 2 3 4 5 6 7 8

Figure 7.10   Coded personal history record.
This form is folded into two parts, with the basic information immediately visible and other information inside. The 1 to 26 scale is used to denote the next salary review. Different coloured signals are used for each half year. The coding 1 to 8 denotes which department of the business the employee is engaged in. For example, number 4 could represent the drawing office (Remington Rand)

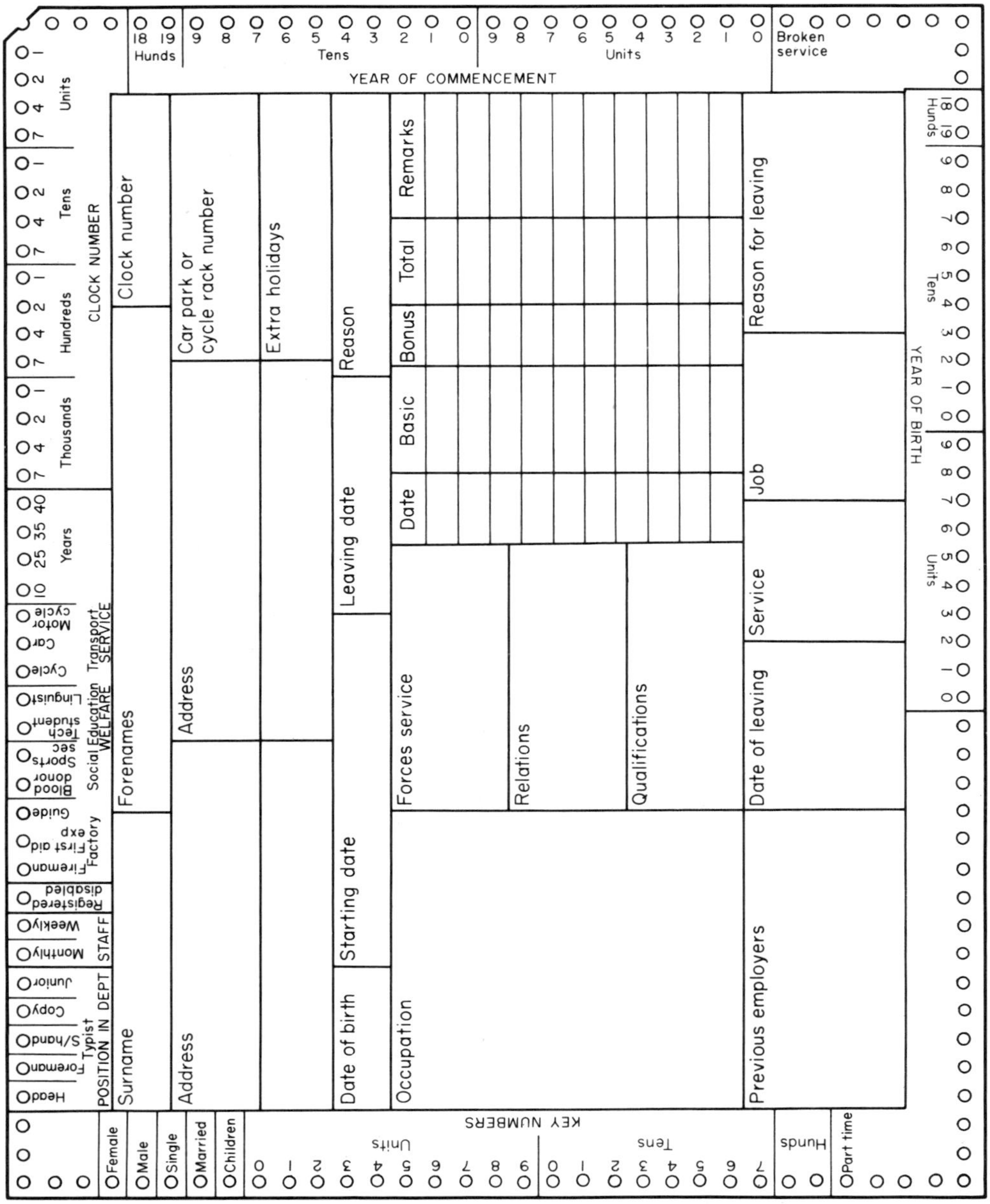

Figure 7.11 Edge-punched personal history card (Copeman-Chatterson).

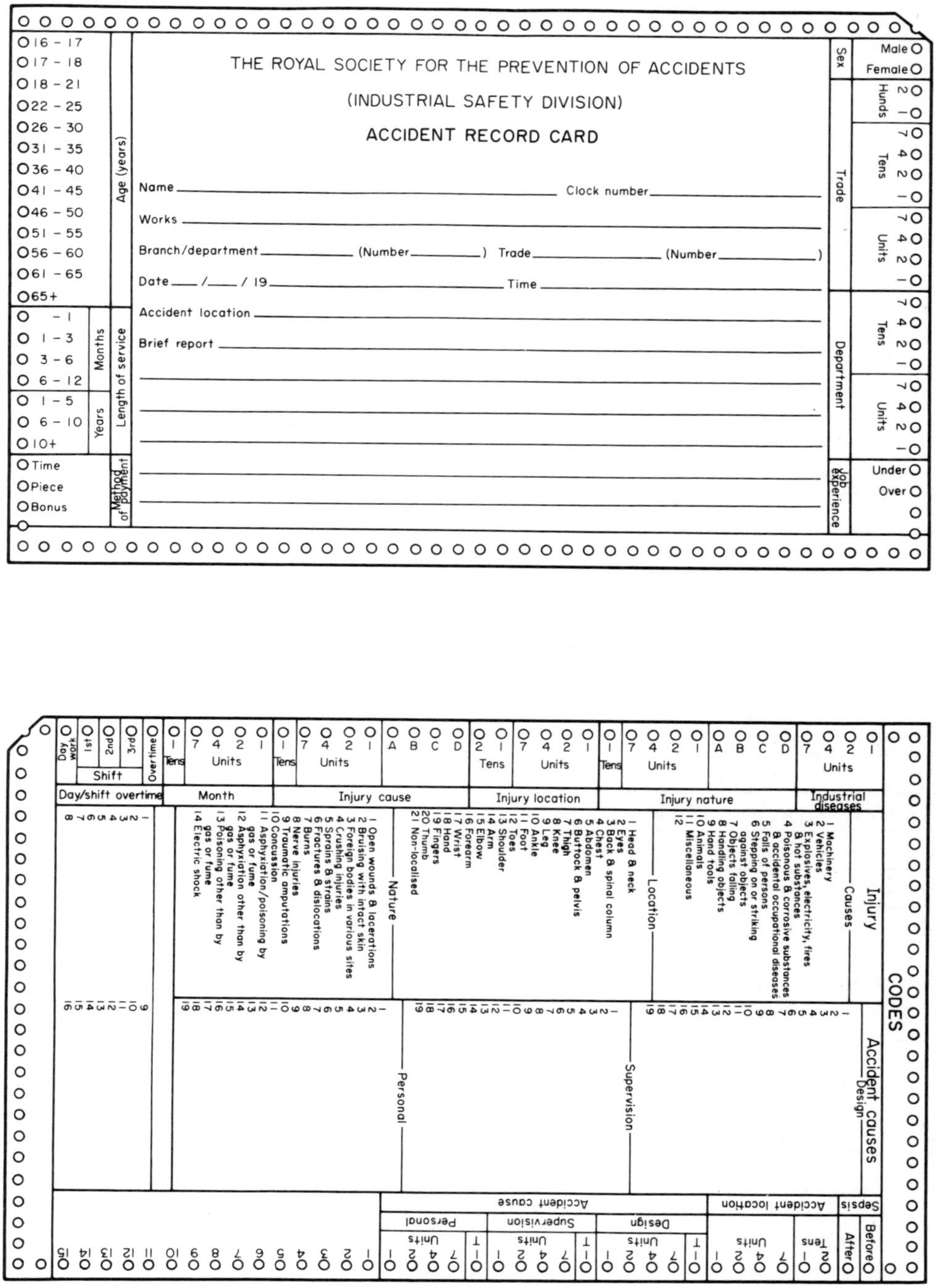

Figure 7.12   Accident record card.
This form is available from the Royal Society for the Prevention of Accidents.
It was designed to facilitate statistical analyses

Name _____ Date of birth _____		
Department _____		
Occupation _____		

Please answer yes or no to all the following questions		For surgery use only. Remarks
Do you suffer from, or have you ever had :-		
Heart trouble of any kind		
Lung trouble (including tuberculosis)		
Nervous trouble (including fainting attacks, fits or nervous breakdown)		
Abdominal trouble		
Skin disease		
Eye trouble		
Ear trouble		
Rupture or varicose veins		
An accident with after effects		
Any other disease, disability or operation		
Has your chest been X-rayed, if so, when and with what result		
Have you lived abroad, if so, where and when		
Are you a registered disabled person		
If so, please state (a) Registration card number		
(b) Date of expiry		

To the best of my knowledge and belief, the information I have given above is correct

Signature _____ Date _____

The information asked for is required in the interests of the employee or prospective employee

On request, an interview with the medical officer will be arranged as an alternative to completing the form or to supplement the information given

Figure 7.13   Medical history form (Marconi Company Limited).

This statement sets out particulars of the terms and conditions on which I (name of employer) am offering employment to you (name of employee) to begin on _____

1 Brief description of employment _____
2 Location _____
3 Scale or rate of remuneration, or the method of calculation remuneration _____
4 Intervals at which remuneration is paid_____
5 Normal hours of work, and any other terms and conditions relating to hours of work _____
6 Holidays and holiday pay_____
7 Terms and conditions relating to incapacity for work due to sickness or injury, and sick pay_____
8 Pensions and pension schemes _____
9 Amount of notice of termination* to be given by_____
                                        (i) employee _____
                                        (ii) employer _____
                        Signed_____ Employer
                        Date _____
*If the contract is for a fixed term, the date when it expires should be stated.

Figure 7.14   Written statement offering redundant workers other work.
This is an example of a form suggested by HMSO. The offer must be made to the employee while he is still employed by the employer and the date completed should indicate this.

8

Wages Administration

An employer must pay an employee as agreed. Employers may request their employees to sign a wages card on receipt of their weekly wages.

Records should be kept showing each employee's gross pay, tax and National Insurance deductions at the very least, and any other details required by the company for administering wages with accuracy and efficiency. Payroll records should be kept for at least two years after the end of each tax year because information may be required by the Department of Health and Social Security or the Inland Revenue within that time. Employers should retain records for all employees who have worked during each particular income tax year, whether or not they are still employed at the end of the year. Pay in any previous employments in the tax year (if known) should be recorded separately.

Deductions from employee's pay

By law an employer is required to make certain deductions, primarily income tax, and may deduct the employee's share of National Insurance contributions. Other deductions, subject to certain limits and conditions, are allowable by statute, such as:

1   Superannuation contributions
2   Retirement annuities
3   Life insurance premiums
4   Mortgage and interest payments

Other deductions which are not authorised by statute may be made, but such deductions must be voluntary and must be paid to a third party. The most common of these are for such things as:

1   Sports club
2   Sickness and benevolent fund, including private health schemes
3   Pension schemes
4   Overall scheme (run by an outside body)
5   Savings scheme
6   Various charities
7   Union dues

It should be noted here that the Truck Acts required the employee's signature for all deductions from the wages of manual workers which are not authorised by statute. The Truck Acts do not apply to non-manual workers, but it is not advisable for such deductions to be made for any employee without his written authorisation.

It is useful to have a composite list of the various voluntary deductions, from which employees can strike out those he does not wish to be made. This list can also be printed on the reverse side of the clock cards as a help in calculating net wages.

In cases where employers supply their workmen with medical attendance, fuel, tools, accommodation and so on, they may make deductions from wages, provided that such goods or services are supplied at cost price and that each worker concerned has given his consent in writing. An employer may not, however, deduct from an employee's pay the cost of protective clothing which the employer is compelled by law to provide.

Calculation of income tax deductions

In order to calculate the right amount of income tax, the employer needs each employee's code number and a set of tax tables, both of which are provided by the Inland Revenue. The tax tables are designed to show the income tax due from an employee at the end of each week or month. Weekly tax tables must be used for employees paid weekly, fortnightly, or at irregular intervals. Monthly tax tables must be used for employees paid monthly, quarterly, half-yearly or yearly.

The employee's code number is shown on the weekly deduction card or the monthly deduction card (P11) supplied to the employer for each employee known to be earning £8 or more each week. These cards are forwarded by the tax office before the commencement of each income tax year (6 April). The code number itself is determined by the tax office and is based on the employee's personal circumstances as reported by the employee himself on his annual tax return. Otherwise the code number is determined by the employee's annual wage, taking into account his own personal allowance.

In calculating the deduction each pay day the employer first adds to the pay due the total of all previous payments made to the employee since 6 April. The Free Pay Table (Table A) provided by the Inland Revenue shows the proportion of the employee's allowances from 6 April up to date for each code number and this figure is subtracted from the total gross pay to date. The resulting figure of taxable pay to date is then found in the appropriate Taxable Pay Table (Table B or C) which shows the total tax due to date on any figure of taxable pay. From this figure of the total tax shown in the table the employer subtracts the figure of total tax already deducted. The remainder is the amount to be deducted from the employee's gross pay on each pay day.

Sometimes (for example, if the employee has worked a short week) the figure of total tax shown by the tax tables may be less than the tax already deducted. In that case the employer must refund the difference to the employee instead of making any deduction.

The wages earned and the deductions made for income tax must be recorded by the employer on the employee's deduction card week by week (or month by month). Space is also provided for entering the employee's graduated contributions (but not the employer's contributions) for National Insurance. If the employee receives a pension this should be distinguished from other earnings.

Returns of income tax deductions

Employers are obliged to make returns to the Collector of Taxes, not later than 19 April of each year, of the pay, tax deductions and graduated National Insurance contributions in respect of all employees. This is done by sending all the deduction cards with a covering certificate (Form P35, Employer's Annual Declaration and Certificate).

On this certificate the employer is required to give the name of every employee for whom there is a deduction card, the amount of the net tax deducted or refunded and the amount of the employee's National Insurance contribution. The figures shown in the tax and graduated contribution columns should be added separately. The total of the graduated contributions columns should then be doubled—to take into account the employer's contributions—and the total entered in the space provided. If an employer finds it unduly onerous to list all the names on the form, he may, by arrangement with the Tax Office, identify the items on Form P35 by numbers, or provide a separate list.

Each deduction card must be completed to show a single figure of pay, a single figure of tax and a single figure of the employee's graduated National Insurance contributions, and any other details regarding superannuation fund contributions, holiday pay, and any other payments for expense or pay from which tax could not be deducted.

The employer is also required by law to give to each employee at the end of the income tax year a certificate showing:

1   The total paid by the employer to the employee during the year ending 5 April and which was taken into account for the purpose of deducting or refunding tax
2   The total net tax deducted
3   The appropriate code
4   The employee's National Insurance number

Apart from tax purposes this certificate is used by the employee for claims for earnings-related supplements to National Insurance sickness and unemployment benefits.

An official form of certificate (P60) is supplied by the Inland Revenue for this purpose. If an employer wishes to use a substitute printed form he may do so if approval is given by the Tax Office. The form must give all the information provided by the official form and the proposed design should be sent to the Tax Office for approval before printing.

National Insurance contributions

An employer should deduct the employee's flat rate and graduated National Insurance contributions according to tables provided by the Department of Health and Social Security. Both contributions are wage related, but the flat rate contribution also depends on the employee's age, sex and marital status. The calculation of contributions is based on the employee's gross pay which is normally the same as that used for calculating income tax.

In general, contributions must be made for all employees in the UK, including those from abroad, under 70 (or 65 for women). Flat rate contributions first become payable for the week in which the employee reaches school leaving age and increases when he reaches 18, when he also becomes liable to pay graduated contributions.

The National Insurance stamps for the employee's flat rate contribution must be affixed on each employee's National Insurance card by the employer. Ordinarily the card must be stamped no later than the time of payment of wages or remuneration for that period. Thus, if wages are paid weekly the card must be stamped weekly. Where wages are paid in advance the contributions must be paid in advance.

There are six types of card, each indicating the sex and age group of the insured person, and the flat rate contribution payable for him:

1   Men age 18 and over
2   Boys under 18
3   Men (special card)
4   Women age 18 and over
5   Girls under 18
6   Women (special card)

The cards for people under 18 are marked *Boy* or *Girl*. Special cards are for the employees who are not entitled or liable to pay the employee's share of the National Insurance contribution or who, being married women or widows, have chosen not to pay.

Contribution cards cover a period of 52 or 53 weeks, and are exchanged annually. In order to spread the work involved evenly over the year, everyone, when first registering for insurance, is allocated and retains permanently one of four different contribution years, beginning in March, June, September and December. The contribution year allocated to a particular employee can be readily recognised both from the symbol *A, B, C* or *D* printed boldly on the card and from the colour of the card which is different for each contribution year. To facilitate stamping, however, the space for each date is in the same position on all cards.

Direct payment methods.   For the convenience of employers there are alternative systems to the use of adhesive stamps for cancelling National Insurance cards.

Employers may, under certain circumstances, use machine purchased or hired from approved manufacturers, for impressing stamps on cards by means of metallic dies. The use of stamp-impressing machines by employers is subject to the issue of a permit, for which application should be made on Form CF 61 which can be obtained from the local office of the Department of Health and Social Security. Payments are made in the normal way, except that units may be set thirteen weeks in advance.

Employers with at least one hundred employees may be granted a permit to pay flat-rate National Insurance contributions direct to the Department instead of using stamps. An application for permission to adopt this system of payment must be made on Form CF 181 which can be obtained from the local Social Security office.

With each payment made at a designated local office of the Department, the employer is required to furnish a certificate of Form CF 189 stating that the remittances represent the total flat-rate National Insurance contributions payable according to his payroll summary or records for all employees covered by the scheme. This certificate should be signed by a director, company secretary or other responsible official.

Under the scheme, the employer continues to hold a card for each employee included in the direct payment scheme. The date of commencement of the permit is entered in a special box (Box S). The employer continues to surrender a card for each employee at the end of the contribution year showing on each card the number and rate of contributions paid and lists these details on a supporting schedule.

Provision of pay statements

At the time a wage payment is made, if not before, the employee must be given a pay statement (often called a wage slip or advice note) showing how his net pay was arrived at. The statement normally shows an employee's gross pay, which may be a combination of his standard pay plus any other earnings, such as bonus or overtime, less any deductions such as income tax, National Insurance contributions, pensions, and so on, and the net amount payable. This saves queries and precludes disputes.

Everyone who has ever been employed in the UK is acquainted with an ordinary payslip. The two payroll statements shown in Figure 8.1 are rather unusual, however, because they are vertical. This makes it much easier to read and, more important to the wage clerk, easier to add and subtract, according to one of the manufacturers.

Kalamazoo claims in fact that the time spent in calculating payroll can be cut by twenty per cent using this format.

Incidentally, full particulars of fixed deductions, that is, the amount of which do not vary from week to week, need not be given with each pay statement provided that:

1   The employer has given the employed person, not more than twelve months before the payment, a statement in which details of each fixed deduction are set out *and*
2   The employer advises the employed person in writing whenever there is a change in a fixed deduction.

The rules regarding pay statements apply equally to payments to employed persons who are ill or working away from the company premises.

Payroll summary

A payroll summary should be maintained as a record of all wages paid and deductions made. Essentially, it should show the gross pay, tax deducted, the total National Insurance contributions and any other deductions, together with cumulative totals. Figure 8.2 are examples of payroll sheets.

In addition, the payroll summary can serve as the basic document for the analysis of labour costs, overtime or productivity measurement, for example, as well as for auditing purposes.

Earnings records

A separate record is often kept for each employee, showing complete details of earnings, tax and insurance contributions, together with an accumulated record of earning and tax over a period of time. This record is obviously useful in providing a complete history of an employee's earnings. Moreover, it is unnecessary, when discussing one individual, to show details of any other individual's record. Figures 8.3 and 8.4 are examples of earnings records.

The earnings record can of course be combined with the employee's personal history record in small firms where personnel and payroll records are kept together. Figure 8.5 shows an example of a personal record containing a record of earnings.

Payroll records showing the total pay, tax and National Insurance deductions for every employee must be kept for at least two years after the end of the income tax year to which the earnings relate.

An earnings record designed to suit a company's own payroll system can, with the approval of an Inspector of Taxes, be used to replace the official deduction cards required under the PAYE scheme. The basic requirement for approval is that the design conforms to the official specification (a copy of which can be obtained from any tax office) and provides the required information, as follows:

1   The whole of the identifying particulars required by the official deduction card
2   Identification of cards for pensioners and directors
3   The total of the employee's graduated National Insurance contributions
4   Particulars of total gross pay and total tax due for the year
5   In the case of an employee leaving during the year, the date of leaving
6   Further information asked for on the deduction card—particulars of superannuation contributions, holiday pay and so on

Where only annual totals are shown, employers must incorporate the necessary figures of pay and graduated contributions in their pay records over the income tax year, supply two copies of their documents at the end of the year and also undertake to keep their pay records for at least three years after the end of the year.

Integrated payroll systems

There are various integrated payroll systems designed to provide entries on each record at one writing. These systems are similar to the multi-posting systems described in Chapter 3. Generally, the payroll summary is placed on top of a sheet of pay slips and each earnings record placed over the payroll sheet in turn for simultaneous recording of entries. The payroll summary sheet is then totalled to give the total wages.

Figures 8.6 and 8.7 show the different types of multi-posting payroll system. The payroll statements in the second system are in perforated sheets while in the first system they come separately. A third system, shown in Figure 8.8 is in fact used for preparing vertical statements. The statements are overlapped with runs of up to eighteen so that each right hand column is exposed. The figures are then added across to obtain the cumulative total of the full payroll. The payroll summary sheet has space for twenty-six weeks of each earnings record.

Standard payroll sheets, earnings cards and pay statements are available in a variety of formats for various purposes. But in each case, the format of the payroll documents used together must be the same for simultaneous completion of entries. Figure 8.8 shows two different formats for payroll summaries and statements each with its own distinctive features. The first is a general layout providing for date, hours and rate at the beginning, basic pay plus bonus, commission, normal statutory tax calculations columns for such things as holiday and sickness payments schemes. The other is similar except that it provides on the right hand side in addition to the net pay a column for non-taxable allowances. This is useful where non-taxable allowances are paid with salary, such as a flat rate car depreciation allowance.

Payment by cheque or credit transfer

Payments by cheque or credit transfer make it relatively cheap and simple to pay wages. Office routines are simplified and the time spend in making up pay packets reduced. Moreover, the employer no longer runs the risk of transporting payroll cash. It should be noted, however, that wages for employees covered under the Trucks Act must be paid 'in the current coin of the realm'. Payment in kind, and this includes cheque, money order or postal order, is illegal without the employee's consent.

Objections to payment by cheque or credit transfer can usually be overcome by employers who are prepared to pay the basic charges of maintaining a bank account. The cost is normally offset against the savings on labour involved in preparing individual pay packets. The co-operation of the unions may also be obtained by arranging for members who have bank accounts to have their union dues paid by standing order.

When wages are paid by cheque, details can be simply entered on individual earnings records, and only the totals for salaries, deductions and net salaries entered in a cash disbursement journal. Multi-posting systems can be used for writing out pay cheques. Sheets of ten cheques are placed over the payroll sheet, instead of the earnings record, and the total amount is repeated in the appropriate analysis columns on the right hand side of the payroll sheet.

With credit transfers, the employer needs to make out only one cheque to cover all wage payments, instead of completing individual cheques for each employee.

Schedules are provided by the bank for completing the payer's name, each employee's name, bank and sums due. If the employee's bank branch sorting code number is known, only this need be given on the schedule in addition to his name and amount of transfer. Quoting individual account numbers also enables credits to be handled quickly and accurately. A suitable authority to cover payment may be incorporated into the schedule, obviating the need to write any cheque.

The auditors may insist that a copy of the schedule be stamped by the bank and retained for auditing purposes. This is easily done either by making an additional carbon copy of the schedule or by taking the cash book to the bank to have it stamped.

The bank distributes the credits through their system. Normally the employees' accounts are credited on the second working day after payments are made by the employer, or the third working day if paid on a Friday or Saturday. If time is too short to use the bank Giro system, wages credits can be sent directly from the employer's bank to employees' bank branches.

The normal payroll records must be kept, even though payments are made by credit transfer, and employees must receive a wage statement each pay day. The name and branch of the bank where the account is kept must be stated on the payroll records, which must indicate whether the account is in the employee's name or in a joint account.

Multi-posting systems can be used to provide bank Giro slips, but instead of a pyroll summary sheet a cash book sheet is used containing details of the bank and branch and the amount credited. A system could be devised so that a tax record card, salary list and individual salary statement, the bank list and individual bank slips are all completed in one posting. For employees on monthly salary, the system also provides an individual earning history and tax record card which can be used for four years.

Computerised payroll services

Smaller employers without computer facilities of their own might consider the feasibility of using time-sharing and other facilities offered by computer services bureaux for payroll calculations.

There are many service bureaux that will take on the entire responsibility for payroll for firms, including the calculation of deductions and preparation of payroll records. The client need give the name of each employee and the basic information only once, including details of bank accounts where credit transfer methods are used. Periodically, alterations are needed, such as the change of tax code number and notices of variants, such as overtime hours or values.

Normally, this type of service is uneconomical for firms with a total complement of less than 80 to 100 employees, although smaller firms may find the cost justified in terms of time saved. Charges usually cover all calculations, plus the supply of completed pay statements, a payroll summary and, if required, credit transfer details. There is usually no charge in respect of programming.

PAY ADVICE			
Week or month number	Date	/	9/4
Details		40 HRS	

	A	20	00
Earnings	B	2	43
	C	1	28
	D		
	E		
	Gross pay	23	71

Gross pay to date	23	71
Tax free pay	9	30
Taxable pay to date	14	41
Tax due to date	3	90
Tax refund		

	Tax	3	90
	Graduated contribution		60
	National Insurance		88
	1		10
Deductions	2		
	3		
	4		
	5		
	6		
	Total deductions	5	48

Net pay		
F		
G		
Total amount payable	19	23

Employer's contribution	National Insurance	3	30
	H		
	J		

Your pay is made up as shown above	MILLER K.E.

Date	
Week or month number	
Details	

	A	
	B	
Earnings	C	
	D	
	E	
	Total	

Gross pay to date	
Tax free pay	
Taxable pay	
Taxable pay to date	
Tax due to date	
Tax refund	

	Tax	
	Graduated pension	
	National Insurance	
	1	
Deductions	2	
	3	
	4	
	5	
	Total	

Net	
F	
G	
Total payment	
Check number and name	

Company's contribution National Insurance		
Selective employment tax recoverable		

Figure 8.1   Examples of vertical statements (Kalamazoo and Lamson Paragon).

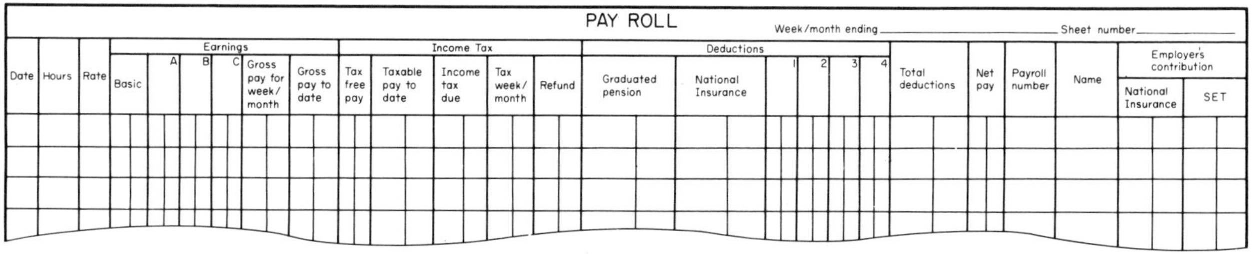

PAY ROLL

Sheet number ___ Week/month ending ___

				Earnings								Income Tax			Deductions										Employer's contribution	
Date	Hours	Rate	Basic	A	B	C	Gross pay for week/month	Gross pay to date	Tax free pay	Taxable pay to date		Income tax due	Refund	Tax week/month	Graduated pension	National Insurance	1	2	3	4	Total deductions	Net pay	Payroll number	Name	National Insurance	SET

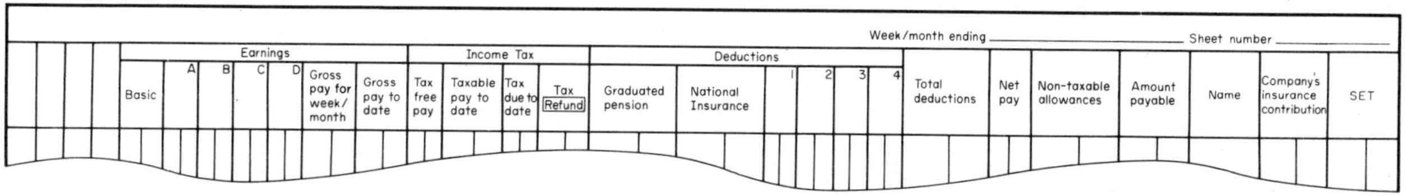

Sheet number ___ Week/month ending ___

					Earnings				Income Tax			Deductions												
Basic	A	B	C	D	Gross pay for week/month	Gross pay to date	Tax free pay	Taxable pay to date	Tax due to date	Tax date	Tax Refund	Graduated pension	National Insurance	1	2	3	4	Total deductions	Net pay	Non-taxable allowances	Amount payable	Name	Company's insurance contribution	SET

Figure 8.2   Payroll sheets.

Two different standard formats, each with its own distinctive features. The first is a general layout providing for date, hours and rate at the beginning, basic pay plus bonus, commission and similar payments, normal statutory tax calculation columns, and provisions for four deduction columns for such things as holiday and sickness payments schemes. The other is similar except that it provides on the far right hand side a column for non-taxable allowances. This is useful where non-taxable allowances are paid with salary, such as a flat rate car depreciation allowance (George Anson Limited).

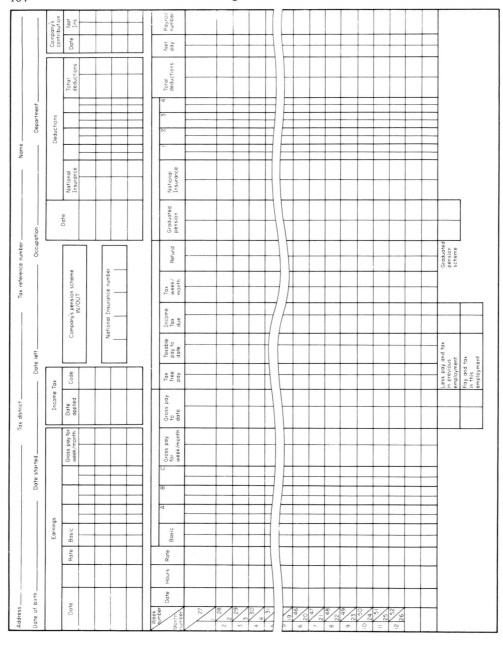

Figure 8.3 Earnings record.
In this layout the superannuation element is deducted from the gross pay before tax is calculated in order to save the need for constant variation of the tax code number. Therefore, instead of having a column on the right of the card for the deduction of superannuation pay, it is on the left between the gross pay and the tax calculations (George Anson Limited).

Address _____ Name _____ Check number _____

Tax district _____ Tax reference number _____ Occupation _____ Date of birth _____

Date of engagement _____ Date of cessation _____ Department _____ National Insurance number [ ][ ][ ][ ][ ]

	Earnings				Income Tax				Other deductions				Employer's
	Date	Rate	Date	Rate	Code number	Date applied				National Insurance	1	2		Nat Ins

Week number / Month number	Date	A	B	Earnings	Cumulative totals					Income Tax refund	Deductions				1	2	Total deductions	Net payment
					Total earnings to date	Tax free pay to date	Taxable pay to date	Income tax due to date		Income Tax	Graduated pension	National Insurance						
						200												
1 / 27 / 1						147 15												
28 / 2						152 60												
2 / 29 / 3						158 05												
30 / 4						163 50												
3 / 31 / 5						168 95												
32 / 6						174 40												
4 / 33 / 7						179 85												
8						185 30												
47 / 11																		
22						261 60												
48 / 23						267 05												
12 / 49 / 24						272 50												
50 / 25						277 95												
51 / 26						283 40												
52																		
53																		

Less:— Pay and tax in respect of previous employment

Pay and tax in respect of this employment

Total graduated pension

Figure 8.4   Earnings record.
Note the strip with figures taken from Table A pasted under the column Tax Free Pay to Date. This form and the one shown in Figure 8.3 can be used for both monthly and weekly paid workers (Lamson Paragon).

Name									
Address						Date of birth			
						Married or single			
						Children			
Education						Date commenced			
						A or *B* list			
Degrees: exams						Tests			
Qualifications									
Previous employers									

Date	Amount of increase	Current salary	Remarks	Date	Amount of increase	Current salary	Remarks

				History					
Date	Division	Department	Job title	Date	Division	Department	Job title	Special gifts

Date	General remarks

Figure 8.5   **A personal record containing a record of earnings.**

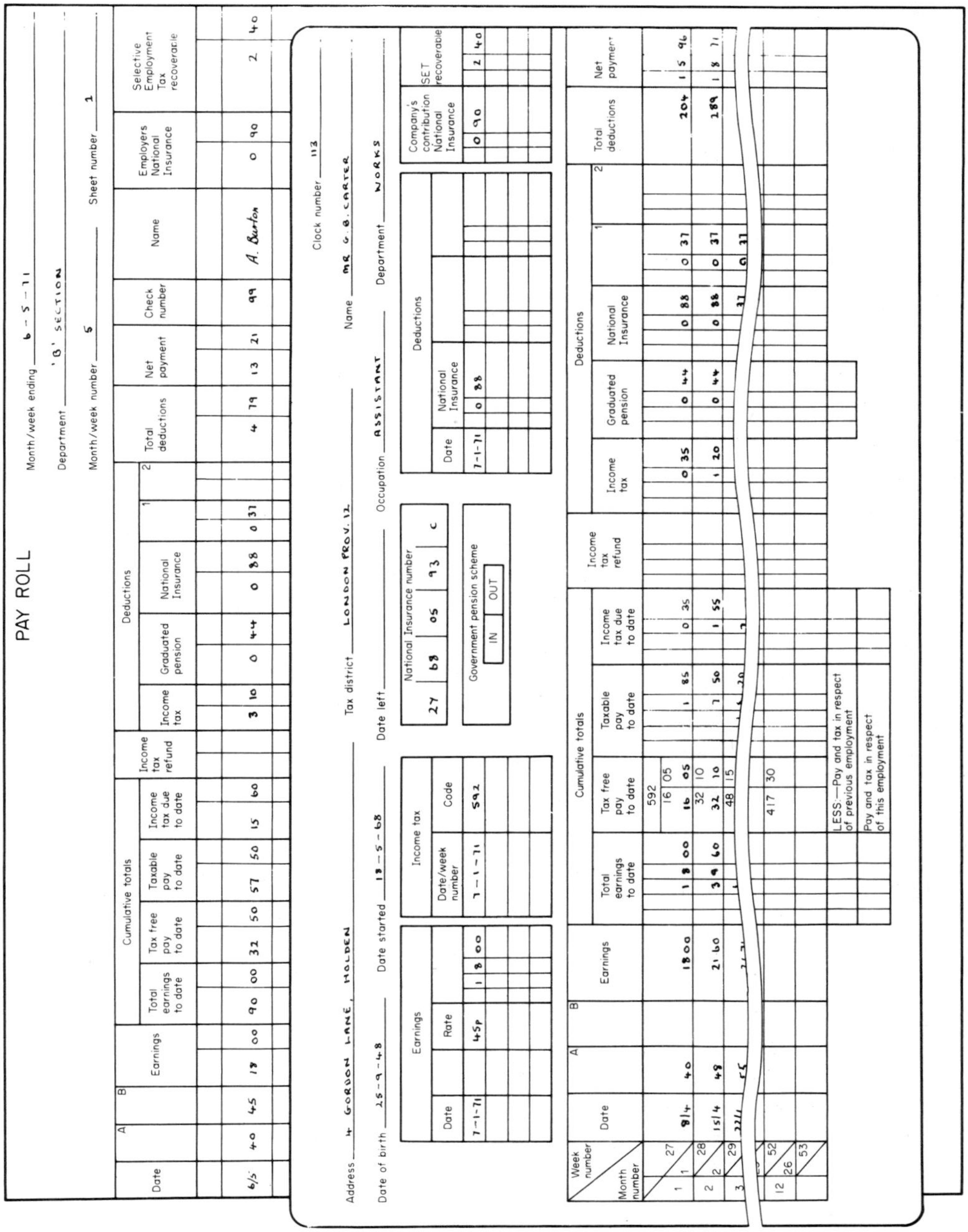

Figure 8.6 Payroll system (Lamson Paragon).

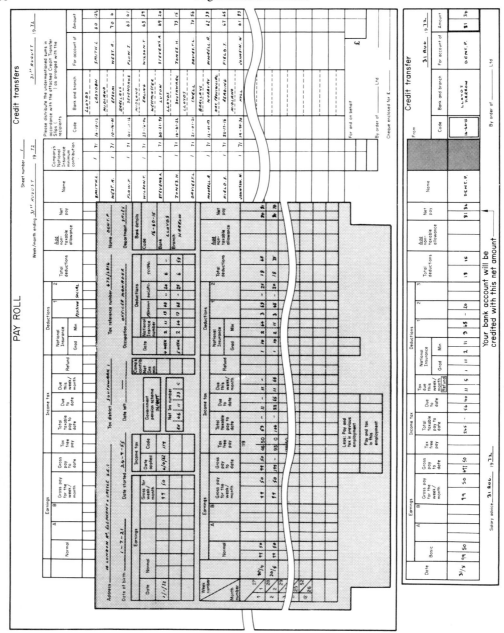

Figure 8.7   Multi-posting payroll system for bank Giro payments (George Anson Limited).

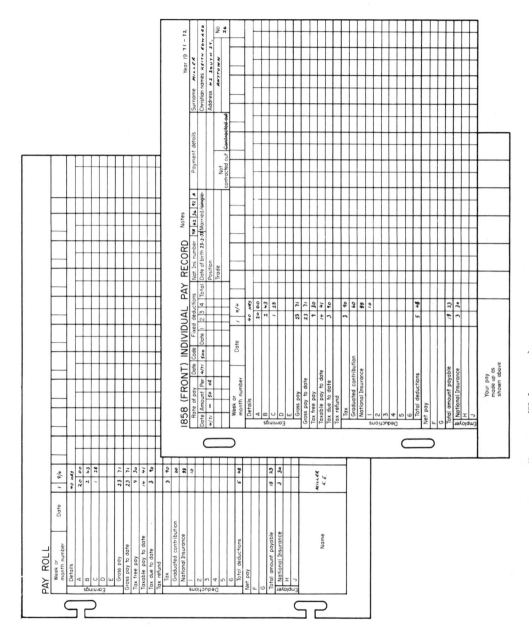

Figure 8.8 Integrated payroll system (Kalamazoo).

9

Maintaining a Records System

The implementation of new procedures is not the end of the story. It is necessary that the established system is properly maintained. It is easy to backslide to the old ways which may have been simpler though less usefull.

Procedures manual and record of forms

A procedures manual should be made available in larger offices, explaining how the records are grouped, what systems are used for indexing and filing each group, their location, the coding structure, the proper procedures for recording data, the procedures for transferring active files to semi-active and storage, and the period of retention for each form. It should also contain an up-to-date list of all individuals in any way involved in the records, and should make clear what their responsibilities are.

It may also be helpful to have a diary indicating when certain forms have to be raised or action taken.

Specimen copies of each form should be kept with the manual. Notes of problems and ideas for improvement can be inserted in a special folder as they come up so that they may be considered the next time the form is ordered.

To facilitate re-ordering of forms, it is helpful to indicate on the foot of the last page of the form, in the smallest available type, the date, quantity and printer. It is also useful to have a record of each form showing quantities ordered and used, frequency of ordering, price, printers and other relevant information. In this way it is possible to keep a control on costs, review the necessity of the form before re-ordering, and establish the most economical order and re-order levels.

Storage and protection of records

There is a need in every company, whatever its size, to protect certain records, either because of their confidential nature or their importance. This includes employees' personal records, references, wage cards, as well as the company's financial accounts. The loss of certain records could be catastrophic to a company.

Every record should be identified in some way as vital, important, useful or non-essential and kept together in files according to category.

There is a wide variety of record cabinets, from fibreboards to metal cabinets. For really vital documents, a company might consider extraordinarily strong files guaranteed against fire, water, steam or violent impact. Ordinary metal furniture cannot stop a fire; it acts as an oven, in fact, and papers can be charred beyond recognition in a matter of minutes in a major fire.

Valuable records should be kept as close as possible to the desks where they are worked on. This will not help to dissuade potential thieves and the curious from attempting to look through the files, but, in the event of fire, the records can be placed under protection immediately.

Whenever a single document is removed from the files, it should be replaced by a substitution card giving basic details of the folder that has been removed, the name of the borrower and where it may be found. The removal of the files should be strictly recorded and spot checks made to see whether any have been taken without authority.

Security precautions must begin from the time any information is committed to writing, however, whether shorthand or other forms of written notes have been transcribed satisfactorily they should be destroyed by shredding or burning. All carbon papers and other types of duplicating paper used with typewriters to produce copies of confidential documents must be destroyed immediateley afterwards. Duplicating machines with meters recording a progressive total of the copies taken will disclose any unauthorised use from a reconciliation of the total of actual copies with the meter reading.

Retention of records

Just how long records should be retained will vary enormously according to the importance of each type of record. Other factors to be considered are space, frequency to which the records are referred, legal obligations, the particular circumstances of the company, the nature of the work, and so on.

It is useful to include a retention period for each record in the procedures manual and to indicate where they are stored. The date for destroying each form can be printed on the form itself in small type. Records can then be filed according to the time when they can be destroyed and a schedule prepared to advise when they no longer need to be kept.

Microfilm record systems

The feasibility of microfilming records for the purpose of storage should also be considered. Microfilming is costly, but so is storage space.

For all practical purposes the term microfilming refers to the reduction of original documents on to photographic film, using one or other of several basic formats. The resulting micro image appearing on the film can be from one fifth to one forty-fifth of the original document size. By reducing the size of documents in this way, considerable storage space can be saved as well as time if frequent reference is made to the material. The main disadvantage is that it is impossible to add documents in their normal filing sequence after filming. It is also difficult to identify different coloured cards, though this seldom matters in stored documents.

Management reports

Too many management reports appear to be designed to do no more than impress senior management with how much information can be compiled. In fact management reports should contain the least information necessary to enable decisions to be made. Indeed, in some firms it is perhaps best not to make any reports unless there is any deviation from the normal.

Informal reports, personally delivered across the desk, are usually more valuable than tabulations of figures and statistics prepared on a regular basis. If data must be presented, it is helpful to summarise the salient features on the top of the report intended for management. Data presented in graphical form can readily convey the essential facts inherent in a set of data which it would otherwise be difficult to appreciate. This can also be done by depicting relationships, such as work in progress to sales of the relationship of debtors to sales, for example.

Listed here are reports which senior management normally find useful:

1   Production returns (quantities and values of production)
2   Production and scrap analysis
3   Packing statement (production packed and ready for despatch)
4   Work in progress (the value of work in progress constituting the cost of materials, labour and overhead)
5   Raw materials, by-products and finished stock statement
6   Hours worked (total number of man hours and cost against the preceding year's figures for each department)
7   Statement of purchase commitments and order position (the value of orders placed for each month, the cumulative value of orders and the cumulative value of deliveries)
8   Sales order position (the value of incomming orders and the moving annual total of sub-orders for the current and preceding year)
9   Statements of outstanding orders
10 Sales and cost value (the value of invoiced sales, the cost of sales and profit by interpolation)

11   Sales forecast (in the light of past experience and in anticipation of current changes)

12   Analysis of debtors

Index